LEADERSHIP WITH A FEMININE CAST

BY: NAIDA WEST

San Francisco, California
1976

Published in 1976 by

R AND E RESEARCH ASSOCIATES
4843 Mission Street, San Francisco, CA 94112
18581 McFarland Avenue, Saratoga, CA 95070

Publishers and Distributors of Ethnic Studies
Adam S. Eterovich
Robert D. Reed

Library of Congress Card Catalog Number
75-41672

ISBN
0-88247-410-3

Grateful acknowledgment is made to the following people: Nancy Valenzuela, who, after her mother's death, gave me permission to quote from the autobiography Green Grows Ivy (1958); Cynthia Epstein, who read and made helpful suggestions about the manuscript; John Lofland, who taught me a great deal about doing this kind of research; Lenore Weitzman, whose extensive commentary throughout the manuscript was invaluable; and Eva Laurin for expert secretarial services. My greatest debt is to the women whose commentary shapes this volume. They gave willingly of their most precious possession -- time -- participating with an eagerness that inspires me to tell their collective story to a wide audience. Their intelligence, wit, warmth, and energy made this an unforgettable project.

In memory of my grandmother,

Elizabeth Simon Smith,

an immigrant of humor, faith, intellect and
fortitude, who, in uncountable ways, continues
to influence the course of life in her chosen land.

LEADERSHIP WITH A FEMININE CAST

This paper reports analysis of data collected by means of interview and observation of fourteen top women leaders in the fields of politics, business, and government. It focuses on background, career development, and leadership styles. The majority of these leaders reported having strong mothers, some economic hardship, and "feeling different" during their childhoods. Most were ethnics and/or were first generation Americans. A process which characterized their divergent careers is described as a spiral featuring hard work, work attraction, visibility, and opportunities. The conditions affecting each of these aspects of the spiral is discussed, emphasizing how they probably differ for women and men. In influencing others, half of the leaders used traditional female kinds of interaction -- either mothering or teaching techniques. The other half modeled their behavior consciously after traditional "male" leadership styles or attempted to use a combination. The mixed-style group reported more problems, which may be described as role strain.

The interviews were designed to probe not only the barriers women face, but also the positive aspects of women's experience. Instead of making the assumption that female socialization predestines women for subordination, I asked if female socialization is an asset to effective management. This interest in the positive direction was rewarded.

TABLE OF CONTENTS

Chapter   Page

PROLOGUE 1

    The Cast 5

    Methods 8

    Qualitative vs Survey Research 9

I.   THE BACKDROP 12

    Strong Mothers 13

        Kinds of Strength 14

        Identification with Mother 18

        Summary 20

    Daddy Needs Help 20

    Stable Families 24

    Praise and Encouragement 26

    Feeling Different 27

    The Family Line-Up 35

    Good Students 37

    Tomboys, Sports, and Gangs 39

    The Lead in the School Play 41

    Few Ambitions 43

    Backdrop Summary 44

II. SPIRALS: THE UNDERSTUDY MOVES UP 46

    Hard Work 49

    Work Attraction 57

Visibility 59

The Big Opportunity 68

    Accepting the Big Opportunity 78

The Lateral Transfer 80

Conclusion 82

III.   THE FEMININE LEAD 85

Type I Style: Playing Mama 85

    Pressures Toward Mothering -- Birth of a Role 89

    Advantages of Playing Mama 91

Type II Style: One of the Men 99

Status Strain: Orphan Annie 102

Summary of Leadership Types 109

    Traits of Type I Leaders 109

    Traits of Type II Leaders 109

    Orphan Annie 110

Common Ground 111

EPILOGUE 117

APPENDIX 121

REFERENCES 128

* ** *** ** *

PROLOGUE

According to most observers, men have a great advantage in gaining acceptance as leaders: leadership is part of the status set of men, but not of women.* In western society "a leader of men" (meaning a male leader of people) is one of the "natural" parts a man may play on the stage of life. It is regarded as bizarre for a woman to play that part. When she takes that part, her femininity becomes suspect. When a man plays that role, his masculinity is confirmed.

To be sure, acceptance of a man as leader is not guaranteed. Studies conducted during the 40s and 50s revealed many facets of leadership, including its problematic definition. George Homans (1950), one of several to attempt a definition, proposed that the leader "is the man who comes closest to realizing the norms the group values highest; this conformity gives him his high rank, which attracts people and implies the right to assume control of the group." Bales' typology of leadership -- instrumental and expressive -- has permeated sociological and psychological literature on the topic. More recently Fiedler and others have sought to define the conditions under which these basic styles are most effective. (Fiedler, 1971) Underlying these concerns is the tenet of Max Weber that all leadership must be regarded as legitimate by followers, or it is not authoritative. (Gerth and Mills, 1969) Seeman (1960) explores relationships between leadership ideologies and social status in the United States.

---

* Merton (1957, p. 370) describes "status sets" as clusters of statuses people acquire, one of which is often "salient" or dominant. Epstein (1971, p. 98) notes that for women, the wife-mother status tends to dominate over career status.

This literature is a useful starting place in analyzing female leadership, and these are some of the ideas around which I have shaped my questions. But the flaw in the literature is that it is peppered with the noun "man" and the pronouns "he" and "him", beginning with Weber's "patriarchal" leader. Excluding women from leadership studies is a serious mistake. Homans' general definition and Bales' definition of "instrumental leadership", for example, may be male types rather than generic forms of leadership. By excluding women leaders from their thinking, sociologists have contributed to an apparent consensus that something in the concept "leader" connotes "male". To put it differently, they inject the status "leader" into the appropriate status set of "man", but omit it from woman's status set.

Do woman leaders acquire the authority to lead in the same way as men? Perhaps there are different sources of authority for women. Can a woman ever come closer to realizing the norms and values of a group of men, than a man? And, if so, how does she get to be one of the boys -- only more so? Or is this necessary? These questions have not been asked, much less answered.*

A further theoretical concern of this paper revolves around the question of status strain. (Epstein, 1971; Goode, 1959) There is often a conflict between behavior expected of women and behavior expected of leaders. A woman manager or politician is said to suffer status strain because she occupies both statuses simultaneously: ideally she should act both submissively and dominantly.

---

* The one sociological attempt to analyze female leadership is Talcott Parsons' treatment of the mother as the "expressive" leader in the family. He does not extend this concept beyond the family. (Parsons and Bales, 1955) Others have. See, for instance, Constantini and Craik. (1972)

Do all woman leaders feel this strain? If so, they might also be classified as marginal, in that they fill a status not normally filled by people who have the status "woman". (Hughes, 1949; Wardwell, 1952) How is the strain or marginality resolved? What consequences flow from it? Do they remain marginal or do they create new compatible roles for themselves?

Individual woman leaders carve out their own styles and their own definition of leadership. Because frequently no socially defined or expected "female" leadership behavior exists in their minds or in the minds of their followers, they operate singly, individually finding solutions to the perennial and universal problem of trying to be effective. They attend schools for management; they read books on leadership; but all of the pronouns are masculine. The suspicion lingers that the strategies effective for men may not work for women.

The women I interviewed expressed these concerns. They volunteered their time willingly because of their keen interest in disseminating information about female leadership. Many of them asked to read the final paper because they want to find out how their counterparts do their jobs. When I asked if they were typical of other woman politicians or administrators, they usually responded as one woman did:

> I have nobody to compare with. There are no women in my
> position at (this organization), and I don't know any anywhere
> else. I know I am different than the male supervisors I have
> known.

While my purpose is to contribute data and some theoretical concepts to the continuing sociological analysis of leadership in different social contexts, it is also to provide practical information to present and future woman leaders.

The paper is divided into sections that focus on the following questions: (1) What socialization did they receive and what motivates them" (2) How did they get there? (3) How do they command respect and authority?

A great deal has been written about the barriers women face. Limits to their advancement in business and the professions are well described by Epstein. (1971) While recognizing these limits, I also focused on the positive side. Instead of asking only "what barriers did you face?" I have asked "how has your experience as a woman helped you?" Instead of making the assumption that female socialization predestines women for subordination and limits them to the helping professions, I have probed the possibility that female socialization is an asset both to effective management and to achievement of such positions. I believe my interest in the positive direction has been rewarded.

Following Klapp's (1965) distinction between symbolic and organizational leadership, an organizational leader exercises authority within a social structure, whereas a symbolic leader exercises authority in the world of meaning or language. With this distinction in mind, I define leadership as the exercise of authority vested in a high position in an organization and the process of influencing group activities. I am investigating leaders with considerable staff or constituents--women whose daily work involves managing groups of people--in contrast to working with ideas, single clients, or data. Although the women I selected to interview are primarily "organizational leaders," some of them have also become symbolic leaders. There are no pure types here, as there are none in any ideal typology.

THE CAST

My first task was to select appropriate informants. I selected them according to the following criteria:

1. Women who direct very large and influential organizations. I wanted top management and successful politicians.

2. Women who had held the position for at least one year.

3. Women in positions requiring working with people more than with written material.

4. Women whose successes were not dependent upon the feminist movement or upon traditional "female" occupations.

My purpose was to learn about the styles and backgrounds of women who had unquestioningly "made it big" in a man's world, at a time when this was highly unusual.

The study took place in California. This proved to be a handicap, for immediately I faced the problem noted recently by the Harvard Business Review (cited in Epstein, 1971, p. 6). There are scarcely any such women available for study. Women I knew about who fit the criteria and who lived in California could literally be counted on the fingers of one hand. I began interviewing those I knew about, and they told me about others.

Of a total of fourteen women interviewed, only seven fully met the first criterion. They direct very large and influential organizations or are elected to important statewide offices. Two of these were assemblywomen, one about to be elected to a larger state-wide office. At the time of the interview, one woman was an elected constitutional officer of the State of California. One businesswoman directs one of the largest commercial ports in California, and

5

another manages and directs the largest toy corporation in the world. One state civil servant holds a key appointive position in one of the largest state departments, and another, in federal civil service, directs one of five of the nation's largest procurement operations for the U. S. military.

The remaining seven women are located at the top in more limited fields or the positions they occupy are somewhat less than top management. Nonetheless, all fourteen women occupy positions that men in their fields would consider very high. These include another procurement director whose organization and budget is somewhat smaller than the one mentioned above, two personnel chiefs who supervise large territories for the federal civil service, one judicial administrator of the largest county in the state, two councilwomen from large cities, including one who narrowly missed becoming the first woman mayor of a major city, and a supervisor of a large county. All of the women interviewed met the second and third criteria. They are organizational as contrasted with symbolic leaders, and they occupy positions usually filled by men.

While fourteen is a small number, it is a virtual universe of people who (1) met the selection criteria and (2) were available to interview. Two top flight businesswomen in Los Angeles refused to be interviewed, and I regret this. One has refused all interviews during her long career, and the other had just decided to accept no more.

Though the women were selected on the basis of their leadership position, there were tremendous differences in power and influence among them. For purposes of sociological study, it is neater to work with a more comparable sample. Had this been a study of male leadership, a more uniform group could have been found, but because so few women in 1974 had held top leadership positions for at least one year, I was forced to "make do" with an uneven group. It should be kept in mind that four of the respondents may be regarded as "middle management" or lower level politicians.* This internal variation in the sample was not altogether handicapping, for I have sometimes used it for comparison when other factors were held constant.

It is of interest to know something more about these women besides their occupations. Ten of the fourteen were married at the time of the interview, two were widowed, one was divorced, and one had never married. Three of the fourteen had no children. The most common number of children was two (six of the women had two children); two women had four children. The average age was between 50 and 51.

Half of the women had graduated from college; five of these also achieved higher professional degrees. Four had only high school diplomas, and the remaining three attended college but did not graduate. Interestingly, all four high school graduates were among the top seven in positions of leadership.

Only two of the women proved to be white Anglo-Saxon Protestants. Most of the other twelve were Catholic and Jewish daughters of immigrants, principally of southern and eastern European origin, or they were reared in distinct ethnic communities, sometimes where English was not spoken. Eleven had fathers who were farmers, operatives, laborers, or owners of very small businesses. Only three of their fathers were professionals -- all doctors.

---

* Since 1974, three of the four have advanced higher or show signs of doing so soon.

7

METHODS

Most of the information presented in this paper was collected by means of taped interviews. All of the women were interviewed. I also directly observed nine of the women as they conducted their business. I was usually a known observer. I supplemented my information about most of the women by analyzing vitaes, published descriptions about the office or business, newspaper articles, and autobiographical materials, published and unpublished.

The first contact with the woman was a telephone call to her office. Sometimes I spoke to her directly on the first or second call. Sometimes I was asked to write a letter explaining my purposes. Occasionally I was invited, at a specific time, to come in to observe meetings or other kinds of interaction at the office and/or interview the woman. Usually I observed one or two days, then interviewed the woman on a different date. Observation was close and intimate in some cases, in the sense that I sat in the office while people came in and out conducting business. Other times observation was more formal: I was but one of many observers at public occasions, such as lectures, meetings, or the like.

Generally, observation supplemented interview materials in the sense that the shortest interviews were supplemented by the most observation. The average interview lasted 1-2/3 hours. The two shortest interviews, lasting one-half hour, were supplemented not only by observation but by analyzing published autobiographical materials. The lengthiest interview lasted four hours. The longest interviews generally took place in homes, where time pressure was less severe.

I also took notes on their settings. I visited the principal places of business of all fourteen women, noting such items as color and style of decor, personal mementoes, seating arrangements, ease of access to workers, and displayed plaques of commendation. This information supplemented what the women said about their style and taste. Besides observing places of business, I interviewed in the homes of five women, noting these items in those settings. I asked the nine women whose homes I did not visit how their homes were decorated, what kind of consumers they were, and what they consider a good life-style.

Qualitative vs Survey Research

To answer the central question -- "What are women leaders like?"-- I feel that the qualitative research approach is most appropriate. There is a virtual absence of sociological information about a "female elite." There is good sociological reason to question the validity of applying information we have about male leadership to female leadership. Therefore, the most basic questions remain open. There is a need for exploration, for asking open-ended questions, and for using data analysis to form the central concepts, rather than imposing preformed concepts on the data. (Lofland, 1971)

Although survey research presently receives more public notice and is commonly regarded as the most reliable way to answer questions about social groups or individuals occupying given statuses, survey research would in inappropriate to the study of female elites at this time.

The most serious difficulty in trying to use survey research would be the inability to frame the most relevant questions for the schedule. I asked all my informants many questions based on the scant literature, mostly from Epstein. I believed answers to these particular questions would be most revealing. If I had designed a questionnaire, these would have been the core questions. As it turned out, I have an entire list of responses to these questions that I have laid aside for future use. They are irrelevant to the body of the paper. They tell little about the women's conduct of business or style of leadership.

The richest source of data came from probing in uncharted directions. Often a woman would remark something almost in passing which, while transcribing, I would recognize as important data -- something reminiscent of something another had remarked. Observation, too, afforded insight that no questionnaire or interview could. This is the strength of qualitative research: It allows for concept discovery.

The strength of qualitative research is also its weakness. I cannot compare my results very well with the results of other leadership studies. I cannot even compare women in high positions with ordinary women or with men. This is often frustrating, perhaps because these comparisons lie implicit in my interest in this subject. Nevertheless, if this paper can contribute a deeper understanding of the world of the successful female leader, perhaps the emergent concepts will form the basis of an adequate comparative study of successful women with both successful men and ordinary women.

I encountered one minor problem in gathering data. Two elected law-makers expressed clear, verbal disappointment when I told them I would protect their anonymity. They wanted their names attached to each quotation.

Sociologists usually study people who want anonymity. It is usually ethical and essential to provide it to them. One hopes to prevent their subsequent exploitation by some more powerful group or individual. One has already invaded their privacy, but to expose them to discomfort or danger would be unconscionable.

Elected politicians, in contrast, are accustomed to invasion of privacy. Answering endless questions about their opinions and life is part of their job. In exchange for this invasion, they receive visibility -- important for spiraling up. (See Chapter II) The two women who expressed disappointment were correct in their assessment that I was proposing to take their time and invade their privacy without giving them compensating visibility. It is entirely possible that the other informants felt the same way, but did not verbalize their feelings. Had I chosen to use names, I might have gleaned fuller data on these two women, for they granted the shortest interviews. On the other hand two women, working in large bureaucracies, gave full interviews, partly because of the promised anonymity. To identify those who wanted publicity would tend to isolate and therefore expose those who wanted anonymity. I chose to make them uniformly anonymous except when a quote from a published source made identification necessary.

Chapter I

THE BACKDROP

How does a woman develop self-definition as a "mover, and a shaker, and a doer," as one of my informants described herself? Sociologists have usually assessed the family as the place that fosters self-definitions and motivation patterns. But most literature on child rearing patterns explains the commonly observed pattern of greater dependency and conformity among girls and women. (Kohn, 1969; Bronfenbrenner, 1958, 1961)

There is some evidence that relates family processes to achievement in girls. Hartly (1959-1960) shows that girls are motivated to work outside the home when their mothers do. Bronfenbrenner writes of adolescents:

> Both responsibility and leadership are fostered by the
> relatively greater salience of the parent of the same sex.
> . . . In short, boys thrive in a patriarchal context, girls
> in a matriarchal. (Bronfenbrenner, 1961:245)

Others have related the matriarchal family to need-achievement in boys. (Strodtbeck, 1958; Rosen and D'Andrade, 1959) My research corroborates Bronfenbrenner's conclusions with respect to girls.

In this chapter I will examine statements the fourteen women leaders have made about their parents and their identification with them. I will also summarize some of the other characteristic factors from their backgrounds -- factors that occurred with regularity. Unfortunately, many interesting but unique stories about childhood experiences must be omitted.

STRONG MOTHERS

Most of my informants unconsciously change the tone of their voices when they describe their mothers. They speak with a kind of reverence. The following are typical responses:

She was kind of a special woman -- strong.

She worked for (a large company), and I don't think they ever had an employee like that. . . . Mother was a very outgoing, competent, intelligent woman.

She's an extremely bright woman from a very cultured background. Big, and strong, and healthy, and bright. Tremendous personality.

My mother was very close (to me). She was very strong, and like the trunk of the tree, as far as the family was concerned.

My mother was an amazing woman. If she made up her mind to go through a solid stone wall, she'd go -- not over it -- not under it! She was tall, erect . . . as a child I was awed by her ability to meet problems head on.

She had terrific values, quiet, but things always worked out for her . . . She was very stable. She got it all together. She was strong in the home. . . . but she was also president of all the auxiliaries and activities.

. . . a very enthusiastic person. . . . very independent. Very creative, very capable, very strongly religious. Mother was the disciplinarian.

What strikes the eye immediately is the contrast between these commentaries and the image of the American woman as the dependent, weak homebody depicted by many people advocating change in sex role typing. Most of the women I interviewed don't understand the poignance of that plea for change, emanating mainly from advocates of the women's movement. They, personally, are not weak and dependent, and neither were their mothers, aunts, and grandmothers. Although they have an intellectual understanding of the problem, their realities don't mesh with it. When they talk of the women in their lives, it is with a candid, deep-felt respect.

Most descriptions of family life 40 or 50 years ago, when these remarkable mothers reared these remarkable daughters, paint a picture of female submission in the family. Male authoritarianism was supposed to be stronger then.*

Kinds of Strength

Frequently the daughters mention that mothers were strong economically or "instrumentally." Mothers worked to help support the family, and in some instances they were the principal breadwinners. The following daughter relates how her mother responded to her father's layoff, due to a mining accident:

> They had a very simple arrangement about insurance and unemployment compensation in those days. If you stopped working, your pay stopped. . . . Everything about her seemed to reflect strength and confidence in an emergency. If there was energy enough for worrying, she would use it instead to meet the problem. (Priest, 1958: 12, 13)

The mother turned her home into a boarding house for miners. The business grew over the years, providing necessary income for the family, whether father was working or not.

> In short order operation boarding-house was going full blast. For the next few years Mother capably ran this growing concern. . . (Priest, 1958: 19)

---

* Edwards, 1969. Several articles in this volume support this theory. See especially J. M. Mogey, "A Century of Declining Paternal Authority", 250-260.

Another informant was reared by an older sister, a mother surrogate. She compares her sister to her brother-in-law:

> She was -- strong. My brother-in-law was quite weak
> (laughter). . . . He was kind of a jolly good fellow
> and was kind of -- strange. At any rate, she would
> work consistently and he would work erratically.

Besides these two mothers who played a very great economic role in the family, three other mothers worked in family businesses, side-by-side and equally with their husbands. Four managed, against great odds, to keep their children well dressed and well fed through the poverty of the depression -- three on farms, one in a city. Their creativity in sewing, gardening, and food management must be regarded as instrumental to the family's well being. Their role cannot be viewed as primarily "expressive," in Parson's sense. (Parsons and Bales, 1955)

The mothers tended to be strong in social and community affairs, too. Sometimes instrumentally strong mothers were also strong in this way.

> . . . Mother always seemed to emerge leader of relief
> activities (when mining accidents occurred). . . . our
> house became the social hub of the town. (Priest, 1958:
> 24)

> She was the advisor for the world. Everybody leaned on
> her.

One mother who was not economically strong emerged as a community leader:

> She is a phenomenal woman. . . . was strong in the
> home, was always home, made us clothes; but she
> was also president of all the auxiliaries and activities.
> She ran for the school board. . . . Our home was a
> social hub. . . .

15

A few mothers had educational and cultural advantages over fathers. In two families the father had only a little elementary school education, while the mother (1) was a school teacher, and (2) finished 8th grade. In two families the mother had lived in America longer than the father and could speak better English. Four daughters mention their mother's or mother surrogate's social superiority relative to their father's.

> I think my father loved Portland. . . . but it was really her decision to go to L.A. . . . she didn't like the fact that when the symphony came to town (in Portland) it had to be held in the (laughter) Masonic auditorium. And she wasn't used to that. She was raised in New York City.

> She's an extremely bright woman from a very cultured background. (Her father was not from such a "cultured background.")

In the following instance the daughter has two aunts on her mother's side after whom she models herself:

> They had gone to college. One was a nurse. I patterned myself after her. They would supplement our cultural lives, buy books. She bought me (laughter) The Last Days of Pompeii. I always remember that.

Another form of mother-strength derives from a matriarchal form of extended family unity. Two informants used the term "matriarchy" to describe their families:

> My grandmother lived to be 99 years old. She stood 6 feet tall and she was a matriarch! Her family is very close. They still gather every Christmas. . . . I'm expected to go with the rest of them. As each sister gets to be the eldest, she gets to be the matriarch. . . . Aunt Mary is 87 now, and she's lovely.

Apparently the above Italian family is not unique. Another Italian informant discusses her concept of femininity:

> In Europe there is a different concept of femininity.
> The women worked hard and were strong. My grand-
> mother was much stronger than my grandfather. The
> mother was the strong one. These families are really
> matriarchal. . . . None of the women in our family
> were submissive. It was the men who were submissive.

Matriarchal tendencies were not confined to immigrant families. The only white, Anglo-Saxon, Protestant, old-family informant describes an incipient matriarchy in her family. One of the first things I noticed in her office was a framed photograph of her large extended family -- her mother's brothers and sisters, their grown children, and their children. In answer to a question about her father's family, she said:

> They didn't have the type of family that we do. . . .
> My mother's brothers and sisters were all raised
> together and stayed together, and still do. . . . We
> (informant and her brothers and sisters) were all raised
> together like that, too.

Notice the use of "they" and "we" to refer to father's and mother's families, respectively. Later when I asked her if she felt the "mantle of the family" were upon her to succeed, she replied:

> Yes. We all did. My oldest brother does not have high
> expectations for his family, and they do not do as well
> . . . that kind of undoes my mother . . . She can't cope
> with it. Mother extends her influence to this second
> generation.

So strong is the matriarchal tendency of this family that even her <u>father</u> "came to think of himself as part of my mother's family."

Besides these three matriarchal families, six others tend in that direction.

> Most of the extended family activity was on my mother's
> side.

17

> Yes, we have a close-knit family. That sister (her
> mother-surrogate) died about 20 years ago. I have
> nieces and nephews by the carload and we're all very
> close. . . . The weight of the world was on her shoul-
> ders. That's the way the weight of the world has been
> on my shoulders.

She is the matriarchal figure now.

> I suppose I identify with my mother's side. They all
> lived there -- my aunts and grandparents. My father's
> relatives were all back East.

Geographic closeness to mother's relatives occurs frequently.

Another indication of mother-strength is the daughter's opinion that

decisions in the family were shared -- that the family was egalitarian:

> I think it was pretty much a shared responsibility. I
> would say decisions were shared.

> When problems came up, or decisions had to be made,
> all three of us (daughter included) "mushed it out".

Altogether these are four kinds of mother-strength. In most families

two or more kinds existed simultaneously. Loosely ranking the daughters by

achievement, I found mother-strength directly related to the daughters'

achievement.

Identification with Mother

The significance of this finding that informants perceived their

mothers as very strong lies in its relation to self-concept. Epstein concludes

that the typical American woman lacks achievement aspiration because she ac-

cepts the social definition of female as having lower capacity. (Epstein, 1970: 51)

My informants accept the status definition of themselves as female, but their

definition -- learned in the family -- is that females are strong, capable, intel-

ligent, and highly motivated.

18

It is usually observed that girls identify with their mothers. (Hartley, 1959-60; Bronfenbrenner, 1961) Thus girls often aspire to be housewives when their mothers were housewives. Epstein wonders if professional women identify with their fathers, who were working models, or mothers, who had unfilled career ambitions. [4] (Epstein, 1970: 80) The evidence of the present research is that woman leaders identify most often with strong mothers. Only three of the fourteen say they "take after" or "identify with" their fathers. These were families that had instrumentally strong fathers. And even these daughters make statements like:

> Values taught in the home were -- respect for parents, particularly my mother.

and another says, "My mother was a very strong person."

Most informants say openly that they identify with their mother, mother-surrogate, or female relatives on their mother's side of the family. One clearly thinks of herself as an extension of her mother's unfilled career ambitions:

> <u>Are you an extension of her -- in what she would like to have done</u>?
>
> That's true. Exactly. I've never thought of myself that way. I admire her as a person. . . . Had she been of this age she probably would be a physician -- she wanted to be a doctor.

The following quotations illustrate conscious identification with mother or mother-surrogate:

> I grew up in a setting where it was normal for the wife to work, and it was normal for the wife to even be a

---

4 Park (1973: 39-57) suggests women who rise to the top may be emulating their fathers.

leader. Everybody came to her, and I think I've sort of taken on the role that she used to have.

She was very strong, and like the trunk of the tree as far as the family was concerned. I would assume that's who I took after, to a great extent . . . I like to think that I am like her.

My mother and aunt were great women . . . My mother had great fortitude. Oh! What she could take! And had to take, too. I marvel at her strength of character . . . I used to say about my mother and aunt (I guess it's true of me, too. I inherited it) "they might be wrong, but they were never in doubt."

Four informants who did not mention specifically that they identify with their mothers appear to have patterned their lives after their mothers, either in being hard-working career women or in involvement in political and community affairs.

Summary

In summary, twelve of fourteen informants had strong mothers in one way or more. They tend to identify with these mothers -- the stronger the mother, the more they identify with her. This has the effect of providing them with female self-images that include the ideas: strong, capable, intelligent -- in short, movers and doers. As one said, "There are doers and there are done fors -- I'm a doer." This is apparently a different view of femininity than the stereotyped American ideal.

DADDY NEEDS HELP

Ten of the fourteen informants either were obliged out of necessity to help their fathers make money or they did it because they enjoyed helping. In this sense, most daughters helped in carrying out the "instrumental" task of the family. They were not shut out of the economic sphere, which is the typical

fortune of girls in our society. Some helped in the store, some worked else-

where but contributed their wages to the family:

> From the time I was a freshman in high school, I used to
> help him make out the bills.

> My mother worked in the store. So did I. After school
> and on holidays. Liquor stores have to be open when
> other things are closed.

> When I was 10 I was taking cash, waiting on trade. . . .
> I worked there during the summer and after school.

> With Dad out of work . . . at the age of 8 I began to feel
> the responsibility of the eldest child and tried to think
> of ways to earn money. (Priest, 1958: 13)

The most successful daughters in my group felt obligated to help the

family make money. Several did not go to college because of their obligation.

But they did not regard this as an imposition or a weakness on the part of their

fathers. "Hard times" and bad luck were responsible. Four daughters mentioned

fathers being disabled or sick for long periods of time. One was an alcoholic,

and the daughter viewed it as an illness. The families of most informants were

severely affected by the depression. These fathers did their best, but were per-

ceived by their daughters as the victims of forces larger than the family.

Three of the fathers were professional men -- all doctors. Are there

similarities between their daughters and the daughters of non-professional men?

One of those doctors feels that he has been drawn into the matriarchal family of

his strong wife. He married her partly because he enjoyed the family -- its way

of living and doing things. He was often gone at dinnertime and in the evenings

because he was the only doctor in town; and while the informant was between the ages of 5 and 9 she never saw him -- he was in the service overseas. Her mother had to be the family leader, and that came easily to her. As a teenager the daughter worked as a nurse's aide in the busy hospital -- the only one in town -- which she calls "his hospital," her father's. In this sense, she helped him in his instrumental role. Although this family was fairly affluent and the father was a professional, there are some important similarities to the poor depression families. Daddy needed help when he was gone; "his hospital" needed help. Father respected and enjoyed mother's strength, and the mother was always the main contact with the outside world of politics and social activities.

The other two doctor families are striking in the way the fathers consciously motivated their daughters to achieve in law and politics -- traditionally male occupations. Both fathers came from Jewish backgrounds and highly valued education. They made no distinctions about what were male and female occupations; they wanted their children to achieve -- male or female. They did whatever encouraging was necessary to ensure their daughters' success.

Although the mothers in these families had only high school educations, they were highly respected within the family. Their daughters regarded them as strong, outgoing, competent, and intelligent. One of these mothers

> . . . thought that the greatest thing that could happen
> to any woman was to have a career. That's probably
> because she didn't have one. My father's feeling was
> that somewhere there was an obligation. I think he
> had a stronger feeling about preparing a daughter for
> independence even than preparing a son.

The other doctor's daughter thinks her parents motivated her to "contribute" to society because they had only girls.

So the opportunities for my parents to have somebody
who could make a contribution had to be with girls.
Therefore I think the same pressures were placed on
me by my family to produce -- to be a leader -- to
participate -- to get good grades -- to go on to higher
education. . . . I don't think it was unusual that I
went ahead and tried to garner this kind of education.

It is interesting to speculate whether the Jewish cultural background
of these fathers contributed to their expectation that daughters could be strong
achievers and, perhaps, contributed to a female-favorable dynamic within the
family. One of my informants -- not Jewish but married to a Jewish doctor --
said she always gravitated toward Jewish boys during her dating years. These
are some of her reasons:

Maybe their mothers told them you don't immediately
start smooching with girls on dates. I always thought
Jewish boys were mother-dominated. (laughter)
Mama's boys. I enjoyed being with them. I didn't
care that they were mama's boys. . . . I enjoyed the
way they treated me. . . . They treated me a little
bit more like a friend.

This woman's mother advised her not to marry an Italian. (She is
Italian.) She says that Italian men try to "assert themselves" in families where
the women are stronger, and consequently they "beat their wives." Apparently
this informant feels that Jewish men don't try to assert themselves in that way
when their women are strong -- and she knew she was strong before she got
married. If Jewish men look upon their wives more as equals and are not as
threatened by strength in women, this may partly explain their daughters' positive
self-images.

STABLE FAMILIES

The bulk of sociological literature on strong-mother families centers on ghetto and black families in which the father is weak and/or absent. These are nearly always unhappy, unstable families. In American society it is often expected that families are happier when the men are dominant and women are weaker in the family. If this is so, it is somewhat surprising that the families of the informants were all stable and nearly all very happy, according to their daughters, in spite of having strong mothers and fathers who needed help.

The families were physically close together. None of the families was broken by death of a parent or divorce. The only time a father was absent for a period of years was in the case of the service doctor mentioned above. Most of the parents worked together in their economic enterprises, whether farm or small business. None of the parents commuted great distances from home. Their residences were near their places of business -- if not in the same place.

Early in my interviewing I realized that closeness of family, in the psychological sense, was important. These informants went beyond giving lip-service respect to their parents. They positively extolled their parents and their families.

> I never felt I was being pushed to succeed. It just
> happened. That's what happens when a kid has com-
> plete confidence and support from the family. . . .
> My father was terribly supportive of everything I did.
> He even carried my school papers around with him
> to show people. He was that proud.

Tears came to her eyes as she described her father and mother. She elaborated key stories from her childhood that taught her lessons she uses today. This is typical of my informants. The lessons learned from their parents' handling of everyday events have stayed with them a lifetime, forming a sort of

encyclopaedia of ethics to which they refer in times of doubt.

We had a <u>tremendously</u> happy home.

But the depression and Dad's illness brought us closer
together as a family than we had ever been. In those
long evenings we spent together -- we had no money to
go out -- we tried to keep each other cheerful. When
the others had gone to bed, Dad, Mother, and I would
sit up late mulling over ways and means to spread the
little bit of money we had. (Priest, 1958: 65) (In some
ways the autobiography of Ivy Baker Priest is a testi-
monial to her family.)

My parents gave all of us a good feeling of self-worth.
"You're really terrific, you've got it! You're just won-
derful. You can do anything you want to do." A positive
thing. Things (bad things) would happen to us, but we
were always bolstered at home.

I had a very happy childhood. . . . filled with swimming,
horseback riding, barn dancing, hayriding, and ice-
hockey watching. It was a very close-knit family, then
and now. (Sacramento Union, 1-27-74:D-6)

(On Christmas) Of course we had accordion, piano,
group singing and dancing, too. Old Italian folk songs.
They were very happy gatherings. No one was praised
greater than anyone else (individual displays of talent).
. . . Oh, my mother was always -- both my parents
were always -- proud of whatever we could achieve.
However, they were very careful not to compare our
achievements against each other -- my sisters and
brother.

In spite of his busy schedule, my father made a real endeavor
to be home for dinner. Dinner was a ritual. We sat at a
table and discussed what was going on at school. And there
was a great deal of interest taken in it. A lot of family conversation, and reports of success were a very important
part of the environment. . . . This was a very stable
family. All the things families are supposed to be.

PRAISE AND ENCOURAGEMENT

Three types of family patterns emerge with respect to praise and encouragement. One type heaps boundless praise and friendly encouragement specifically upon these daughters. These daughters achieve and are most glowing in their reports about their parents and childhoods. A second type encourages all the children as a group, but does not single out individuals for special encouragement. These daughters achieve, remember their families with great warmth, do not care that they were not specifically encouraged; they seem to step easily into a female leadership role. A third type does not praise or encourage the children -- especially not the girls. The daughters do not remember happy homes specifically, though they do not label them unhappy. They resent the lack of praise and encouragement. One suspects their achievement is a kind of reaction against being ignored.

> I had no direction, no discipline. I had no pat on the back for winning swim meets. Everything was on my own. I used to ride my bike miles to compete in sports. . . . Never received any encouragement. Nobody drove me, nobody clapped, nobody said "go." Every single thing I did on my own.

> At term end you would stand up if you got an "A" and everybody would clap. That was very encouraging. I wanted my mother to come to the ceremony to see it. I also had lead parts in the plays. But no, she would not come. And father never had anything to do with school.

> Was femininity stressed in your family?
> I had little parental direction of any kind, in femininity, school, working, or anything.

Again, these latter comments represent a "minority report." The second type is numerically the most common among my informants. When I probed these women about the lack of specific encouragement, they had no resentment. They had happy childhoods; and they feel whatever their parents did was natural. Their parents had imparted guidelines for successful living which the daughters have put to good use. They feel the general, all-around supportiveness of their parents is largely what put them where they are today.

The three types of families hold together when grouped by socio-economic position. The daughters who received the most specific praise and encouragement came from professional and middle class backgrounds. The ones who received no specific praise and encouragement were daughters of less well educated farmers, laborers, and small businessmen. There appears to be no difference in the achievement of women who resented the lack of specific encouragement and the ones who did not. Apparently specific praise and encouragement are not necessarily part of the background of successful woman leaders.

FEELING DIFFERENT

Unfortunately I did not ask all the informants if they had felt different during their childhoods. Most volunteered it, and two fully explained its effect on them in terms of their achievement. Four informants talked about their childhoods in such a way that I inferred they felt different from the average child. I concluded only one informant did not feel different. Together, nine of fourteen informants talked directly about having felt different; five talked about it indirectly; and only one did not. Ninety-three percent of the informants felt different during their childhoods. In contrast, in a previous study, I asked a sample of preschool teachers and aides (nearly all women) the questions "overall my life experiences have been fairly average" and "there is something in my background that sets me apart from the average person in my position." Only 18% (N=143) "felt different" as measured by their answers to these two questions. (West, 1971) Clearly, feeling different characterizes these fourteen women leaders but not preschool teachers. The following are some ways in which the leaders felt different:

> I was brought up in two different faiths. I had formal education in a Jewish Temple and in a Catholic convent. . . . I was one of the few non-Catholic children in the school. I couldn't participate -- or didn't participate -- in many of the religious events. . . (and I sat) through doctrine class, although (I was) not given the credit for it.

The following quotes come from women who felt extremely poor and poorly clothed during childhood:

> Perhaps the childhood ridicule we suffer toughens us and increases the ambition to amount to something. At any rate, in my daydreams I saw myself achieving fame and fortune in the outside world and returning triumphantly to the old home town, to the blare of trumpets and cheers of crowds. I'd be a stylish lady, of course. . . (Priest, 1958: 37)

> I saw all those bright kids who won the popularity contests, honor rolls, etc. Being first generation Italian, I had the feeling I was not wanted; people looked down on us.

> I felt bashful and somewhat different than the rest of the kids due to my parents' fundamentalist religion.

Two informants felt different in having been relatively well off in poor neighborhoods. An immigrant from England says:

> The other kids called me "maudy baby" -- like "sissy." Also, I had nicer clothes, since we were better off and lived in a very poor neighborhood. . . my father believed in saving his nest-egg.

The following table shows the extensiveness of ethnic and immigrant factors in informants' backgrounds:

28

National Origin of Family		Religion--Parents/Grandparents
American 3 or more generations	3	Protestant/Protestant/Catholic
Russian	2	Jewish-Catholic/Jewish
England/Scotland	2	Mormon/Protestant
*Italian	2	Catholic/Catholic
*Bohemian	1	Catholic
*Poland	1	Jewish
Germany	2	Catholic/Jewish
*China	1	not ascertained

*Foreign language spoken in the home.

First generation immigrants -- 7
Born in the United States -- 13
Born in England -- 1

Numerically and socially, protestantism dominates the United States. Only a small proportion of these fourteen women leaders had a Protestant background. However, religious differences in themselves were generally not the source of the informants' childhood feelings of being different, though two mentioned religion in this context. The most commonly mentioned source of those feelings was ethnic and immigrant status of their parents. Besides seven first-generation Americans (first generation born in the United States), two second generation daughters lived in non-English-speaking ethnic communities with grandparents and other relatives who were immigrants. These two women felt the same immigrant ties, or effects of those ties, that the seven immigrants' daughters felt. Nine of fourteen woman leaders with definite ethnic and immigrant ties was a surprisingly high percentage. If Jewish background is included in "ethnic," then ten, or 71% had ethnic and/or immigrant background. This emerges as one of the most interesting findings of this study.

Two informants mentioned economic differences between themselves and their neighbors as the main source of feeling different, but economic position was clearly related to immigrant status. Together six women leaders of fourteen felt different during their childhoods due to ethnic and immigrant status of their families. The question must be asked: What is the relationship between immigrant ties and leadership in women?

I was not the first to notice a high proportion of first generation Americans among successful women. Cynthia Epstein (1971) found that many woman lawyers between the ages of 40 and 50 years had immigrant parents. She interpreted her finding in this way:

> Immigrant parents might be more apt to encourage
> daughters to try a new way, and to find a better life
> in the new world, than old-stock American parents
> who are rooted in the structure as it is or who are
> too tradition-bound to expect change. (p. 78)

This interpretation rests on the theory that change takes place when the bonds of tradition loosen. According to this view, immigrants were jarred loose from traditional role conceptions, either because of their uprooting or because of culture clash. In either case, daughters would be freer to develop positive self-images than old-stock American daughters.

I probed the possibility that my informants were not given traditional feminine training. All but one (the most outwardly "feminine" of the group) said they had received fairly extensive training in feminine manners, speech, activities, and dress. They felt no differences in their upbringing, in this respect, and the "average" girls' upbringing. I found no evidence that immigrant parents encouraged their daughters to "try a new way." These daughters of ethnics and immigrants were not encouraged nor did they feel a compulsion to become "new women" in the new world. While there are problems of comparative validity in using self-reporting as a means of analysis, these reports suggest that the achievements of the ethnic women should not be described as a loosening of tradition or a liberation from the old. What appears, instead, is that in adherence to tradition, they missed the training in submission and inferiority that attaches to female status in America, but not in other places. In nearly every case they followed the example or the advice of their relatives in matters of female behavior and manners. Achievement motivation, strong in American culture, was very strong in immigrant families. As girls, the ethnic informants never felt achievement should be restricted to the male sex. Achievement among these women appears to be an expression of strong American and family values, not a breaking away from tradition.

Immigrant daughters had a belief in their capacity, while native American girls apparently tend to accept society's definition of inferior female abilities. As an alternative to the "breaking loose" hypothesis, it is possible to explain female achievement as an ancient cultural pattern not fully eradicated in parts of Europe.

Pre-Roman Celtic culture, widespread throughout Europe, may have featured strong women who were heads of households and leaders in economic, military, and political affairs. (Davis, 1971)* According to this view, male-dominant, patriarchal social forms have not fully replaced earlier social

---

* For instance, Tacitus' description of Celtic women. (From Davis, 1971: 212)

patterns, especially in protected rural areas. Just as modern religious festivals contain many survivals of pre-Christian beliefs, so might belief in female capacity in those areas stem from earlier norms of female leadership which was related to the widespread belief in a female diety.*

The following quotes nicely summarize the sentiments of immigrants' daughters on the subject of femininity.

> In America women are taught to wear frilly clothes and be passive. I believe femininity means a sense of gender. I know I'm a woman. I don't have a conflict about what is feminine and what is not. It doesn't threaten me to hold public office. Everyone has to learn to do it with grace and sensitivity. Those are human qualities.

> I am a woman. I'm very pleased to be a woman. I wouldn't like to be a man.

Independence -- an important component in the motivation of these fourteen woman leaders -- is valued highly by immigrants' daughters. The following quote adds to the interpretation that female independence may be part of family and cultural traditions, not a breaking away from family tradition:

> My grandmother never did want to come (to the United States). She made my grandfather unhappy some of the time. For instance, she wanted to see the Panama Canal. So she left to see it. She said if all these kids can't take care of him, something is wrong. (14 children) My grandmother went off to more places than you can imagine! In those days, when traveling was difficult.

---

* In this context, it is interesting that in "backward" rural Albania more than one-third of the elected representatives of the Peoples Assembly are women -- a very high proportion for Communist or Western nations. In rural Serbia today, according to Goode (1970: 34) families of marrying girls feel they ought to be compensated for the loss of a working member. There is ample evidence that this attitude is a survival from an earlier period, and I would argue the attitude of viewing women as economic producers is not unrelated to female achievement.

Notice she worries about the children's ability to take care of her husband, rather than the other way around. The woman who related the above story highly values her personal independence, apparently continuing a family tradition.

Further evidence that achievement of first generation daughters is an expression of old traditions rather than a discovery of new ones comes from responses to the question about whether the "mantle of the family" was upon you to succeed.

> Yes. The old feeling that you had to go out and bring respect and admiration for the family. That's the old way of expressing it.

The following quotes demonstrate family influence upon the informant's achievements:

> . . . the parents came here to build a new life, and it's a very restricted life. . . The first generation felt this.

> The opportunities for my parents to have somebody who could make a contribution had to be with girls.

> . . . if there is such a thing as immortality, it is that they (parents) are in me.

In achieving, these first generation daughters were carrying on a family tradition or fulfilling a family hope with the redoubled vigor of a child who sees beloved parents living poorly in the land of promise, or saint-like parents whose influence was restricted.

If the fact of family immigration was not responsible for their positive definition of female status or motivation to achieve in the first instance, what was its connection to acquiring leadership positions? I believe it intensified a family or cultural motivation to achieve and, very importantly, increased the likelihood of their learning certain important skills.

> The parents of other kids had already exposed them to
> different community activities. The door was already
> open. . . . I had to make my <u>own</u> openings. It is hard,
> and you're young. So you start formulating your own
> <u>ways</u> of how to get into the groups or organizations.

She continues:

> I think you learn early in life to analyze things. . . .
> You realize "I must learn to speak on different subjects"
> and "I've got to be able to present myself in this type
> of a manner."

As a consequence of feeling different, she consciously learned the skill of pre-

senting herself in strange environments. That skill proved to be invaluable in

her male-dominated business career. In combination with her ambition to

achieve, her intelligence, and her positive self-image, this girl's social skills

gave her the means to overcome sexual barriers and achieve to the highest degree.

Another immigrant's daughter feels her success was partly due to her

childhood desire to "overcome."

> I think I had a double thing to overcome. Not only did I
> have the immigrant parent background, but I was being
> raised by a sister and brother-in-law. The need to sup-
> port myself was with me all the time. Not that they made
> me feel it. They were extremely generous. But I felt
> the compulsion.

The desire to overcome negative social evaluation of one's status un-

doubtedly played an important role in motivating several of these women. And the

interpersonal skills they learned probably played an important role in their ability

to reach their goals.

Interestingly, the two women who felt different on account of being

relatively well off in comparison to poor neighbors are now primarily in the busi-

ness of helping poor people acquire jobs and education. The two who felt different due to economic deprivation now regularly handle money in the millions of

dollars. And the four who suffered most from ethnic slurs now make laws.

THE FAMILY LINE-UP

Birth-order studies usually reveal that, in terms of creativity and

leadership, first-born children have an advantage. (Epstein, 1971 p. 78) But

most leadership studies have been of men. Epstein suggests first-born girls may

be under greater compulsion to conform to traditional feminine pursuits (See also

Kammeyer, 1966: 508-515). According to Kammeyer's reasoning, last-born girls

have the advantage of being freed from traditional role expectations, which operate

against achievement.

Thirteen of fourteen informants in this study were either first-born or

last-born -- seven first-born, six last-born. Only one woman had a different

placement in the family. She was fourth of five children. There was no relation-

ship between ultimate success and first as opposed to last position in family.

Neither does that factor divide them by occupation. The sole mid-family woman

is one of the least successful by the high selection standards of this study.

A first-born woman explains her feelings about the effect of birth

order:

> You might find that oldest daughters are the achievers,
> too. I had to give my parents the kind of satisfactions
> that they would have gotten from a son, since it is so
> important to have a son. I took responsibility. My
> mother had lots of responsibility, too. I grew up with
> a tremendous sense of responsibility.

A last-born opines:

> The youngest is more like a grandchild. The difference
> in age between my mother and I is tremendous. My

older sister was more like a mother. You get spoiled.
You have more than one mother. You get to go with
your brother, your sisters, your parents. . . In my
generation, the eldest banded together to push the
youngest through with education.

Another last-born says:

I got the best end of the deal. By the time I was in high
school my parents were traveling; I got included -- the
others didn't. I got a car -- they didn't.

Kammeyer's reasoning may explain the large percentage of last-born daughters, but not the first-born. He concludes the traditional female sex role, internalized more often by first-born daughters, is the submissive, helpful, wife-mother role. There shouldn't have been any first-born daughters here. However, he also concludes that first-born daughters are more likely to agree with their parents about the feminine role. If one remembers that the feminine role in many of these families was instrumental and socially forward, then Kammeyer's theory may hold. These daughters were following in their mothers' -- or female relatives' -- footsteps.

One may wonder if preponderance of first- and last-born children is an artifact of small families -- families of one or two. The mean number of children in the families was four. Five families had three or less children; four families had five or more. They ranged from one to ten children. Considering the number of children per family, birth-order information becomes more interesting. Apparently some kind of selection favors first- and last-born daughters in achievement of success and leadership. The two most successful women in the group came from the very largest families. One was the eldest of seven; the other was the youngest of ten.

GOOD STUDENTS

Edwin Lewis's exhaustive review of scholastic achievement concludes:

> Scholastic comparisons between boys and girls reveal
> that girls are superior in almost all aspects of academic
> achievement. . . They enter college with superior high
> school grades and continue to do comparatively well in
> college. (Lewis, 1968: 45)

In this respect the fourteen woman leaders were typically female. Most of them say they always got good grades in school, though they did particularly well only in subjects that interested them. Two mentioned being school valedictorians. Only one of the fourteen was conscious of "toning down" her grades to gain social acceptance. The others "knew what I meant" by that, but enjoyed and sought achievement anyway.

Interpretations of girls' comparative superiority academically usually start with their greater verbal facility, due to differential socialization. (Lewis, 1968) But frequently those interpretations include variations on the theme that girls have a better attitude toward school. Teachers like them, they are better behaved, and they conform to academic values presented by the teachers. Drews (1961) writes:

> Achievement in terms of grades may be partially due to
> the fact that most girls accept the values of the school
> and, at least to an extent, identify with teachers where-
> as many able boys do not. (Quoted in Lewis, 1968: 47)

My data show these women leaders have great respect for learning and for people in positions to teach them, if, indeed, the two can be separated. If this respectful attitude is termed "conformity," then the evidence supports Drews' conclusions. The fourteen women leaders often expressed their orientation to learning, and they expressed it in many different connections. Rather than say they achieved because they were smart, they say they had the desire to learn. They also have a humble attitude toward books, teachers, and mentors at work. In no instance did they mention breaking with tradition or the way their various teachers wanted things done.

It is difficult to separate childhood from adult attitudes toward learning.

> I have spent my life making up for what I missed by not going to college. Anything I have done, there has been a lot of reading attached to it -- to do a better job.

> I tried to learn all the regulations. . . I had respect for the regulations, the people there ahead of me . . . I was the outstanding student in the (management) school.

> The impact and importance of education was always brought home to me in the home.

> We had an educationally oriented family. Education and careers were extremely important. . . . I recognized what people said; that you weren't to be better than boys . . . but that's just never really impressed me as being a valid argument.

Referring to improving her performance in her present position, she thinks of books:

> If you know of any good books on administration, let me know . . . I don't know if that's because every business is different (the fact there is little information on techniques of administering). Anyway, I'd be interested in source material.

> Being Jewish was always a plus to me. . . I had that extra. For most first and second generation Jews, the most important value was that their children be educated. I inherited that.

I questioned a woman about whether she "got a lot" out of business school. I had guessed, since she was already very successful in business, she might have had the view -- as many men do -- that experience teaches more than books. Her answer reveals a deep respect for academic learning:

> Oh, yes. I was like a person thirsting in the desert without water, who suddenly finds a water hole and can't get enough. (In the entrepreneural class) there were 50 men and me. I got so much out of it! I used to go to the library and load up on books. Work around the clock -- read all night . . . I learned as much in that two semester thing -- once a week -- as most people learn in a full career (laughter) -- in a full educational program.

One woman had the experience of attending management classes during her rise in an organization. Her immediate superior scorned her respectful attitude, saying techniques learned there were valueless. He told her, "that's a bunch of bunk!" She never forced the issue but, now that she has his position, she employs those techniques to the great advantage of the organization, she says.

Respectful attitudes toward authorities, books, teachers, and learning in general typify all the woman leaders. If, as Lewis suggests, their propensity to "conform" academically is due to female socialization, we may assume these women experienced typical female socialization in that respect, and further that, female socialization may be an advantage where achievement depends on schooling.

TOMBOYS, SPORTS, AND GANGS

I asked one informant if I had left out anything important in the interview. In answer, she stressed the importance of competitive sports in preparing women for competitive occupations in adulthood. Women, she said, are usually unfamiliar with the language of competition. They feel uncomfortable challenging others. They do not put themselves into challenging positions. She, in contrast, was accustomed to sporting competition.

Checking back, I found I had neglected that area of questioning, but some informants had volunteered it. Subsequently I inquired specifically about sports and was surprised to learn what a role they played in the youthful and adult lives of these women leaders.

All of the women I asked about it talked fondly about their love of sports and their early participation in competitive events.

> I played state championship badminton (in school) and volleyball. I was a professional swimmer for a year. I play tennis now.

> I like sports, too. I played golf. After I won a few trophies, I quit (laughter). I really ran out of time.

> I was an avid horseback rider for most of my youth. I rode in various equitation and other competitive events. Then I became a golfer, and for a while did a good deal of swimming. Now I'm enmeshed in tennis . . . Athletics played a major role in my life.

> It happened I was a very good football player and that distressed my father very much. For years I didn't get an allowance because every time my father came home and caught me playing football with the boys he took my allowance for a month . . . I could throw a ball and kick a ball farther than any other kid on the block . . . I play tennis medium well.

> I was one of the boys. Baseball, football . . . I was a real good catcher on the baseball team. Then I joined the girls' baseball team in high school. I enjoyed sports. I learned how to use a gun when I was nine years old . . . I used to walk eight miles to school. After school I'd play about an hour of tennis, then walk home. I had a lot of exercise . . . I was familiar with competition from a very young age.

> I could never get close to girls the way the other girls did. I liked the boys a lot. I used to relate to the boys. I was quite a tomboy . . . If they'd play basketball or whatever they'd do, when they'd let me, I'd run with the boys . . . I didn't like dolls.

> I enjoyed playing with the boys, their games. We had a
> baseball team. We had to make our own entertainment
> around the ranch, so girls and boys intermingled.
> <u>Did you like to win?</u> Oh, yes.
> <u>Did you win?</u> Oftentimes (laughter).
>
> Anything I ever did, I wanted to win. I was a tomboy. I
> ran around with large groups of kids, boys and girls,
> packs of us.
>
> . . . fellows and girls were all the same, playing together.
> We played baseball, football, kickball -- anything. I had
> all boys next to me (in age) . . . I had to play with the
> boys!
>
> As I grew into adolescence, I was imbued with the notion
> that, to win the esteem of the opposite sex you must be
> able to excel at their own games. (Priest, 1958: 33)

And they have -- all of them -- bested the boys at their own games.

Familiarity with competition may prepare girls for competitive occupational situations in later life. Playing with boys may be an independent factor in that preparation. As girls, most informants learned to see themselves as "one of the gang" -- of boys and girls. They did not experience the inferior status definition inherent in segregation. An elected administrator describes the lasting effect of integrated play:

> It didn't seem to anybody that you were being too much of
> a tomboy in our little mining town . . . boys and girls
> together. I grew up in that kind of atmosphere, so that
> I never could quite separate women's this and men's
> that -- to me we're men and women working together.
> Just like when we were kids, we played together. I
> never did favor women's divisions. You don't isolate your-
> self -- you become part of the whole.

THE LEAD IN THE SCHOOL PLAY

Leadership potential typically expressed itself early. It is characteristic of them to have been president of school clubs and organizations, whether academic or athletic. Two mentioned being captains of debate teams; one was vice-president of Stanford University. Ethnic status sometimes interfered with full development of potential:

> I always wound up president of everything as a child and
> in high school. I never meant to do that; it just happened.
> I would join the organization. Problems would come up.
> I would talk too much, and wind up president.

In college, she encountered some barriers:

> The school was run by fraternities and sororities. Obvi-
> ously I didn't fit there, being Jewish. But everything
> else -- I was president of the Jewish Club, and other such
> things.

> I joined things in school and often became president or got
> other offices.

> As assistant editor of the school paper, captain of our
> debating team, member of the student council, and lead
> in the senior play (she finally achieved happiness in
> school despite earlier awkwardness and insecurity).

> I was always chosen for parts in plays. The lead part in
> the senior play. Maybe this is just the way I am.

> I also got the lead part in the school play.

Only three of the fourteen informants reported not having been leaders in school activities. Two of these did not go to college, which may explain their lack of participation.

The pattern seems to be, for most, a period of early insecurity related to "feeling different," and finally a blossoming as leaders. The two who did not attend college had not yet overcome their insecurities. The most common achievement was the great honor and visibility of being given the feminine lead in the school play.

FEW AMBITIONS

Almost all of the women say they are surprised to have achieved as much as they have, considering their low aspirations early in life. Only two are now doing about what they planned early in life. The planners and non-planners share an attitude toward work and independence which is probably related to their success.

> As a young child, I could hardly wait till I was 21 years of age and could earn a living. I didn't see myself as anything -- I just wanted to earn my own living! . . . I didn't want to depend on anybody.

Did your first husband object to your professional life?

> . . . I needed to be my own person. I needed a sense of independence and direction in my own life. He needed someone to complement his personality -- to be the traditional wife, half-person kind of thing. (Earlier, she said, she wanted to "put as much distance between herself and the housewife image" as possible.)

Most of the women in politics now, whether elected or appointed, began working for causes. At first they found personal satisfaction in volunteering their services. Eventually their status changed. The following woman speaks of the change.

> I suddenly woke up one day and thought, "I'm grown up now, and there isn't any daddy, and I guess I know how to do it as well as anybody, or better." That was a terrible revelation. It's hard growing up. You want to believe that someone else is always taking care of things . . . I became the state coordinator (an election campaign).

Whether they began as salaried employees or volunteers, the women enjoyed working. They are surprised to be where they are today, because they lacked aspirations, and some continue to lack aspirations. These are very typical responses from women in civil service and politics, respectively:

I've never looked ahead to say that -- as a matter of fact
I never even dreamed I'd be the director . . . I don't
see myself better than my clerk-typist.

What do you want to do in the future?

I feel I've got it made right now. I just love what I'm
doing. Every day when I get off the elevator I just grin.
I love working . . . Ten years ago I wouldn't have believed that I would be here.

It may seem surprising that these women achieved so much with so

few ambitions.* I believe their achievement is related to a remarkably common

philosophy. It revolves around doing the best job you can where you are. A poli-

tician says it well:

I have always felt I was at the apex of my career, no
matter what I was doing . . . My philosophy is to do
the very best job at everything that I can. Nothing is
too trivial or menial if it's something that has to be done.
I take pride in my work.

BACKDROP SUMMARY

The high achievement of the women analyzed here often begins in a

childhood setting that combines (1) emulating effective, vibrant mothers or female

relatives who were mother-surrogates, (2) taking the role of assistant to fathers

-- sharing the instrumental role, (3) being part of close-knit, supportive families,

(4) feeling different from other children, (5) overcoming negative evaluations

outsiders ascribe to their families or wanting to increase the sphere of influence

of loved, but restricted parents, (6) learning the manners, dress, and outward

---

* Tausky and Dubin (1965) show that only one in ten American managers in
bureaucracies are future oriented. In this respect, women may not be different
from men.

activities of female status, but also learning to play with the boys and compete in athletics, and (7) achieving scholastic and social honors early in life. They value doing a good job where they are and tend to have few ambitions.

How do women who tend to have few aspirations rise to the top of their fields? This question is the focus of Chapter II.

Chapter II

SPIRALS: THE UNDERSTUDY MOVES UP

On the surface it would appear that the career developments of these fourteen women have little in common. The diversity is striking but not prohibitive to analysis. In this chapter I will describe what appears to me to be a spiraling process of career advancement that is common to all informants, and to connect the stages of the career spirals with conditions that appear to unlock advancement from one level to the next.

One manager had advanced in a single organization in which she worked for 31 years. The politicians seemed to be swept into office the first time because of a combination of flukes and favorable circumstances. Two administrators had been appointed to high exempt civil service positions after having been housewives for many years. How can these disparate careers be compared? What do they have in common with the career of a businesswoman?

There are vast differences among my informants in how their successes were achieved. They were promoted, elected, appointed, or self-propelled. Within the promoted group, there are personal, structural, and situational differences in promotion patterns. This is true of the elected group. Personal, party, and situational differences account for their successes at the polls. In private business personal, structural, and situational factors account for success or failure. But what of citizens appointed to top level administrative positions? What structure were they part of prior to the appointment? What situations among hundreds can be selected as the relevant ones for answering the question: How do women rise to the top of the political and occupational career ladders?

The first step in seeing a pattern common to all the informants is to erase the artifact of salary. Perhaps it is true that salary, more than any other work-related factor, divides men from women in much of what goes on in America. There are women at work everywhere, developing careers -- perhaps unknown to themselves -- for no money at all. The patterns of their careers may well be identical to the patterns men experience, but we are often blind to the similarity because we are accustomed to drawing a sharp distinction between paid and unpaid work. The two exempt appointees, housewives according to the press, in actuality received the logical and typical career reward for years of hard work in a field.

Having removed salary, I could see that all the women informants followed career advancement patterns of a similar broad nature. At the bottom, or entry level, the person's sphere of influence is narrow. Therefore the lowest level of the career spiral is small. (See Chart, p. 48) As development proceeds to the next level, influence broadens, and so forth to the top, where it is very broad. Therefore the spirals are drawn like upside down, graduated springs. Note that the spirals are of different sizes. After reaching the top of a spiral, a woman may make a lateral transfer to a larger one in order to broaden her sphere of influence. This pattern may describe the careers of men and women, though the processes within the pattern probably differ.

The internal processes that determine whether a woman moves up to greater influence appear to be: hard work, work attraction, visibility, opportunities, and hard work at a higher level. These "stages" are value-added. Hard work is a necessary condition for work attraction but it is not the only condition.

47

Chart 1

CAREER SPIRALING
In the Worlds of
Politics, Business,
Government

Organization with Wide Influence

To History-
World of
Meaning

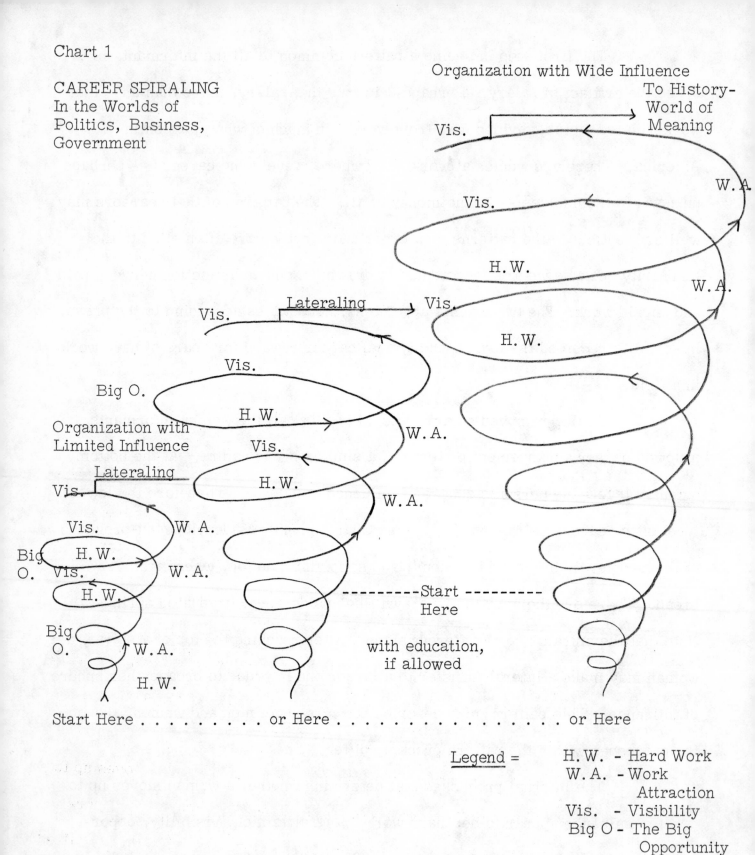

Organization with
Limited Influence

Lateraling

Big O.

Vis.

H.W.

Vis.

H.W.

W.A.

W.A.

Vis.

H.W.

Vis.

H.W.

W.A.

Lateraling

Vis.

Vis.

Vis.

W.A.

Big
O.

H.W.

Vis.

W.A.

H.W.

Big
O.

W.A.

H.W.

----------Start----------
Here

with education,
if allowed

Start Here . . . . or Here . . . . or Here

Legend =

H.W. - Hard Work
W.A. - Work
         Attraction
Vis. - Visibility
Big O - The Big
         Opportunity

48

Hard work and work attraction are two necessary conditions for visibility, but there are others; and these three factors, along with others, are requirements for the big opportunity. Accepting the big opportunity is, of course, the main requirement for appearing on stage II, ready for more hard work at a level of greater influence. The process begins anew.

HARD WORK

Do women work harder than men for equal rewards? Overwhelmingly the women responded in the affirmative.

> I did more and was willing to do more. If that meant coming into the office on Saturday or Sunday . . . I just assumed I'd do it.

> They'd give out ten contracts. I'd take my ten and get them done. Then I'd go back to the boss and say, "Now is there something else I can do for you?"

> I was working with men; anything they were expected to do, I was expected to do. The only thing I used to think was that a woman, to keep ahead in her job, had to do three times better than a man . . . I really worked for what I got. In 1952 my mare was foaling, and I didn't know it for three days because of working overtime.

In a newspaper profile of one of the politicians I interviewed, a reporter summed up the commentaries about her, made by colleagues and other acquaintances:

> Tenacious, hard-working, energetic, hard-working, diligent, hard-working, full of spunk, hard-working. Hard-working. *

After a frightening trip in a small plane on a stormy night, one woman was asked by a male companion if she were not especially afraid when she

---

* Sacramento Union, January 27, 1974. p. D-6.

discovered the pilot was a woman. She retorted, "on the contrary, that was the most reassuring thing that happened. Let me tell you, young man, a woman has to be twice as good to earn half as much at anything as a man." (Priest, 1958: 256) The year was 1957.

Simply working hard isn't enough, according to one woman:

> I worked harder (than others). I was effective . . . It
> isn't a matter of how hard you work. It's what you
> accomplish! Some people work hard, but they don't
> really know where they're going.

There is almost unanimous agreement among the informants that upward moving women work harder and accomplish more than their male colleagues. There is no unanimity about the reason for it. All of the women working in bureaucracies, whether they were appointed or promoted, describe the motivation as internal, rather than externally imposed on women as a group.

> You set your own level of work . . . (It is) what you're
> willing to achieve. If you didn't want to bother with
> (a difficult kind of work) you could just never be
> available.

> I did more in order to get ahead, and I think by my
> doing more I raised my own standards. They measured
> me by my overproduction. Maybe that's where a person
> would get the idea that standards are higher for a woman.

This point is made by several women. The standards are their own. A consequence of wanting to learn more about the job causes them to do more work than other employees, male or female. But their promotions were related to their overproduction.

In politics there are less well-defined work standards. There is also some ambiguity about what kind of work is appropriate. Most of the elected politicians discussed this ambiguity. One widely held opinion among politicians is that an effective lawmaker is one who gets his or her name attached to "major legislation." The people for whom major legislation is being written live all over the state. Thus "work" means relating to the State as a whole and to others whose focus is broad.

All four elected woman lawmakers choose what they say is a less popular and more demanding definition of their work. One calls it "scut work." It involves responding primarily to constituents. It means trying to answer every phone call, every request for speeches, and every demand.

> Every piece of correspondence that comes into my office that's an original, I see and I personally dictate an answer to.

Showing that this approach to work was not traditional:

> When I came on the board I don't think many supervisors answered their mail. Now I think that's changed.

Some colleagues of a statewide legislator have called her "ineffective" because she spends her time on little issues. She responds:

> What is government but a response to the people's needs and the people's wants? . . . Our day-to-day lives are more affected by the little issues than the big ones . . . I think it's important to get involved in legislation people do understand. *

Another says:

> I have very close feeling to the counties I represent. I feel strongly that you have to pay more attention to legislation that comes through here to watch how it might affect my district.

---

* Sacramento Union, January 27, 1974. p. D-6.

A colleague of hers remarks, "because her philosophy is to represent the little people . . . many issues here (the Legislature) are not big ones in her district; she may take a different view."* Generally, attention to little people or little counties does not lead to popularity on a statewide level. Though recognizing that it may be so, these women continue working long hours for those little people.

> My day begins at 5:30 a.m. and goes often till 1:00 a.m.
> Constituents call me at home. Sometimes I feel perhaps
> I should tell them about my hard work, but the old saying
> is that if you don't like a job, why seek it? I love mine.**

The fourth lawmaker was less sure about the kind of work she should do to be judged good. I asked her how she rated her ability.

> I don't think I'm a good politician. I don't know how to
> rate my ability. Is it in terms of how often you speak
> out? how many things you push through? how many
> you propose? I don't know what people consider
> effectiveness.

She continues:

> I think I am effective in being responsive to my constituents.
> People never have problems getting through to me.
> . . .
> I feel I have the European work ethic . . . Maybe I work too
> hard.

In contrast to the women in bureaucracies, four of the five woman lawmakers feel external standards are imposed on them -- standards that require harder work for women than men. In response to these standards they do ever

---

* Sacramento Union, January 20, 1974. p. D-7
** Sacramento Union, January 20, 1974. p. D-7

more "scut work" or work for constituents.

> The public expects higher standards because I am a
> woman. Not my colleagues. (Colleagues don't have
> higher standards.)

The standards she refers to relate to integrity. However, this informant says

women politicians have "worked hard to prove themselves" honest and dedicated.

One politician feels the people who supported her for office are the

ones who impose higher standards than they hold for men.

> There was an important decision to make last year. I
> felt I didn't have enough information to vote on it. You
> should have heard the repercussions! I never heard
> anything like it. My best friends called me and said they
> were very unhappy about my abstaining. I said, "Why?
> X abstains, Y abstains. What's wrong with abstaining?"
> . . . But they said, "It's different with them." . . .
> They want me to be above reproach and maybe it's because
> they worked so hard to get a woman elected, they don't
> want anybody to criticize her.

The press also criticized her.

> I wrote (to the paper) saying, "They hadn't endorsed any-
> body for President, but when I abstained it was female
> indecisiveness." . . . I feel that more is expected of me
> and I think that's unfair. When I campaigned I said, "I
> will never make a decision without fully understanding
> both sides." That was my own high standard. They ad-
> mired me for that when I was campaigning. (laughter)

Another informant believes high standards are imposed by curious people or con-

stituents who did not work for her.

> They often express shock: "You really are all right."
> Or "We're watching you." . . . I'm overly prepared for
> the agenda every time because all these people are
> watching. I want to be very prepared because of that . . .
> I agonize over appointments because it reflects back on
> me.

Another woman says that people who support a male lawmaker don't expect to agree with his decisions 100% of the time, but --

> People (especially white, middle class people who supported me) will expect to agree with me 100% of the time. When I cast a vote they don't like, they are much more depressed than they would be with anybody else.

What Are the Conditions for Hard Work?

Whether high standards for work are their own, as the bureaucrats feel they are, or imposed from the outside, all the informants say they have always had an ability and a desire to work hard. Even the political women who said high standards were imposed from the outside also describe themselves as hard workers by nature.

> When I start doing something, I go hog wild on it. My workday never ends. That's why I like politics -- you're always working on it.

> Whenever I saw something that needed to be done, I thought I had to do it . . . I always have to be accomplishing something, no matter what.

> I am not happy unless I am really working.

> I drive myself very hard.

Besides a penchant for it, stamina and strength are additional conditions that make hard work possible. This may seem surprising in view of the fact these are "desk jobs," but often these jobs entail working very long hours without rest and under great pressure.

One woman compares her stamina to that of men who held the job previously:

> Sure, I do (work harder than men) . . . But you see, I have a capacity. I am quite unique in that. I am a

tremendously healthy person, with a profound amount of
vitality and vigor. I've never been sick in my life . . .
There have been men in this job who -- well I would almost say they were infirm.

Her capacity makes her work harder.

I have a capacity to do -- both physically and mentally --
so I have a sense of commitment that I should do. And I
do!

Several other women concurred that they had been tremendously

healthy all their lives, and that in part accounted for their rise to the top. Other

people comment upon their vigor.

Some people have told me that when they first came in
they thought, "she goes by nervous energy." It's not
nervous energy; it's just tremendous stamina.

Most of the women mention good health as essential to doing their work. Several

said they are healthier working than they would be otherwise.

I was sickly as a little girl. (But) my health is better
now than it's ever been. I thrive on responsibility and
work . . . I know I can run the whole (military department) with no problem.

(I'm) very healthy. No ulcers, blood pressure. I find
it's easier on my health to be a chief than to be an
Indian. Physically, the most trying condition is frus-
tration--not having authority.

I think if I were back home (housewife), I'd have more
to worry about.

Two of the fourteen women have had health problems related to pres-

sures of statewide and nationwide political campaigns. One collapsed after

holding a national cabinet-level directorship while caring for three young children,

worrying about household matters, and touring the nation on a full schedule of

appearances and speeches, day and night.

> (People would tell me) "this is a killing pace . . . when
> you get out of here, you'd better get some rest." But I
> was on my way to Tampa, wondering whether (husband)
> would remember (daughter's) appointment with the dentist
> and whether he'd gotten the washing machine fixed.
> (Priest, 1958: 254)

> There were breakfast and luncheon talks, and "could you
> just drop in to our reception for a few minutes?" and
> then a campaign speech before two thousand in the civic
> auditorium. (Priest, 1958: 255)

The other woman now suffers high blood pressure acquired during a

campaign.

> The toll of that campaign cannot be measured. On my
> birthday I dragged around L.A. trying to get an organi-
> zation together, yapping on phones. I had the flu. But it
> had to be done.

Ivy Baker Priest, terminally ill and in pain at the time of the inter-

view, continued administering her department and performing the ceremonial

speech-making required of a person in her position.

Stamina and good health appear to be important conditions for hard

work in high level positions. Ability is another essential condition. And if

women work harder than men, then more stamina and more ability are required

for women in high positions.

A third condition for hard work comes from the structure itself. I

have in mind, simply, that organizations that enforce rigid rules of work appor-

tionment will not have some employees doing hard work while others at an equal

level do little. Perhaps no such rigid work structures exist. It may be a uni-

versal fact of life that some people work harder than others, and that organiza-

tions give their implicit sanction. All the organizations investigated here

sanctioned work inequalities.

WORK ATTRACTION

It is easiest to see the connection between work attraction and promotion in the federal civil service, where the process is institutionalized. In other organizations the same processes operate, but they are unofficial or informal. Work attraction is the gravitation of work toward individuals willing and able to do it. It is analogous to the pull magnets exert on iron filings. In the federal civil service, job descriptions are accompanied by the phrase "and other duties as assigned." This phrase gives sanction to work attraction. Regularly, personnel inspectors review each person's work load for the express purpose of changing that person's classification (rank and pay) if the work load has increased in scope or responsibility.

All the women I asked (13 of 14) agreed strongly that capable people do more. A personnel chief says:

> Efficient people attract work, get loaded down, are
> evaluated yearly, and reclassified if necessary. Less
> efficient people have little to do.

The four women who were promoted from the bottom to the top ranks in bureaucracies say their love for learning was responsible for work attraction. As typists, they wanted to learn about the regulations. As supervisors, they wanted to learn about management, and so forth. Apparently there is always unattached work available for interested and willing people to do.

> I wanted to learn different kinds of work. They would
> give me something else to do (when she asked) . . . I
> ended up doing my (work) plus the different work they
> gave me . . . I think the inspections and ratings were
> fair in that they gave me credit for what I did.

The political women acknowledge a work attraction phenomenon, too.

> I've had constituents say, "Give it to (me), she'll do it.
> So I agree, people who can do work attract it. I'm a
> doer.

In volunteer groups, where politicians begin their careers, work attraction is operating.

> I usually wound up fund raising chairman (sic) of every
> group I was in . . . If you give any inkling that you are
> interested in something, you end up being chairman.
> That's what happened.

This woman qualified her statement with the observation that it also takes demonstrated ability to become chairperson of organizations.

The obvious limiting condition for work attraction is the rigidity with which organizations define work loads. The work attraction phenomenon occurred most markedly in organizations that were relatively unstructured and informal. Perhaps this partly explains the faster gains up the career spiral in politics, as compared with bureaucratic careers.

Though it is less marked in civil service, the structure allows work attraction. This phenomenon in civil service somewhat contradicts the Weberian notion of rigid work apportionment in bureaucracies. Ideally, according to Weber, positions in bureaucracies are assigned according to the outcome of prior tests of merit. Thereafter work is distributed according to standardized rules. In actuality, if the lives of the women studied are representative, people everywhere in bureaucracies are doing work not specified in their job descriptions. As managers, most of the informants continue the practice of using people to do jobs not specified by their official job descriptions.

> There are no sharp lines between line and staff here.
> It all depends on who can do the work. It has nothing
> to do with official job title.

Looking back over her rise in politics, an elected administrator muses about how certain people are selected to do jobs.

> You're thinking of someone to do a job, and you think, "Oh, so and so could do that!" Why? Why did you decide that? There's just <u>something</u> about that person.

In her own case, when people asked her to do jobs she felt incapable of doing, she remembered the advice of her father, who said, "Of course you can do that! They must have thought you could do it, or they wouldn't have asked you."

In summary, the hard workers I interviewed attracted work beyond what was normally expected. This attraction of extra work critically shaped their careers and was limited, but not prevented, by the amount of flexibility of the organization in which they worked.

VISIBILITY

To be successful, it was not enough to be a hard, efficient worker, and it was not enough to attract more work. These facts had to come to the attention of people in positions with authority to promote or advise. This was true in bureaucracies, in politics, and in other work settings. Visibility, then, means gaining the recognition of important people in terms of the positive effect their support will have on one's future. Sometimes having done a good job is enough.

> Again, the most successful thing is to get recognition. To achieve recognition. Then I think all those artificial things disappear (female stereotypes). You don't know they exist.

> The more you do, the more you come to the notice of those who think you can do more. More people are saying, "She can do that."

I showed enough strength in that race to bring me to the
attention of others in the party. Soon after I was elected
co-chairman of (political organization). (Priest, 1958:
87)

In politics the critical people are the voters and party leaders, and

the gate keepers of visibility are the press. One politician weighs the importance

of visibility against working hard to understand the issues. This is an unusual

juxtaposition of these two factors. Usually hard work brings about increased

visibility, but in this instance it did not.

Maybe I worked too hard to find answers before meetings.
I found that sometimes I would be too quiet at the meetings
because I felt I already understood everything. My interest
wasn't visible. You have to make your work visible to get
any kind of credit.

Apparently recognition is no unproblematic consequence of hard work. Woman

politicians may also get visibility for the wrong reasons. They often claim to get

recognition for less important work.

The press will look for the off beat. One of my greatest
disillusionments is that I can work for a year on a project
-- tax reform or something really important -- and the
press will not pick it up as being anything that gets more
than a line in passing, but you do something like liberate
a restroom and it becomes very pressworthy.

Being treated unfairly by the press was mentioned by one informant as a common

complaint of about a dozen councilwomen in California who met for the purpose of

discussing that problem. The informant tells me:

I have come to the conclusion that they don't want me to
show up too well (laughter). I feel a little immodest
saying that. I asked (another councilwoman) what she is
doing about it. She said, "I just send out a newsletter
telling people what I'm doing. That's the only way they'll
find out, if I tell them myself."

60

It appears that the elected informants have turned their attention to "scut work" and complete accessibility as a partial solution of the visibility problem. Although that kind of work requires more energy, it apparently compensates to some degree for the lack of press attention.

> The first time I ran and came in first was a little bit
> of a fluke. The second time I don't think it was a
> fluke. I think it was a product of four years of this
> kind of one-on-one service to people.

Thus, perhaps, choosing the more difficult and unreported work with constituents may have the function of providing woman lawmakers a personal visibility in their districts in the absence of the press recognition, which they believe is accorded unequally to their male colleagues. While none of the informants reported this connection specifically, I think this interpretation is tenable.

Epstein (1973: 26) has written that women rarely rise to managerial positions because men already in those positions do not commonly view women as management potential. Women do not get the eye of "gatekeepers." She may be correct in her analysis. The women I talked to did get the eye of these "gate keepers," but these occasions were mentioned as the important turning points in their careers.

The following story illustrates the importance of recognition by a superior in advancing from clerical to managerial positions. One woman entered a government bureaucracy as a typist but advanced rapidly due to "wanting to learn more," work attraction, and reclassification. She says that when she approached the top of the clerical spiral and was about to take an exam for the highest clerical position, a male supervisor took her aside and said, "don't waste your time; the grades for stenographers are limited." He advised her to take the exam for managerial grades, which she had thought were reserved for college graduates. She passed, and was on her way into management.

The other three women promoted upwards in government bureaucracies also began as low level typists, but achieved managerial levels during World War II before the separation between clerical and managerial work was institutionalized. Testing makes promotion from clerical to managerial work more difficult. Today clerical workers may have the same reservations about their ability to pass the test as the woman quoted above. But even before the formal separation of management levels, women required the recognition of superordinant men. One says:

> It was quite obvious that the director favored me over anybody else . . . He didn't use much wisdom. I was only a 7 (grade 7) and they (her immediate superiors) were all 11's, but he (the director) would ask me to do special things (work beyond that which her job required). And after two months I got a promotion.

Her rapid rise in the organization brought about lasting jealousies on the part of supervisors who are now her subordinates.

Another woman names a high placed director as the most important turning point in her career.

> He took a fancy to me, I guess because he liked my work. . . . He told me once, "You were the only one that really had the potential. You really were concerned about your career."

He sent her to the right schools, made sure she got copies of all the latest materials -- "the things you don't normally get unless somebody directs you." After he had groomed her thoroughly, she said he made it a "point to expose me."

These three women had attracted different kinds of work than their job descriptions stipulated, because they became visible to men who groomed them for administration. The fourth woman promoted in government bureau-

cracies does not mention specifically the tutelage of a male supervisor. She

took over the management of a division soon after it was formed during World

War II. The division grew, as did her job description, and she was accorded

the appropriate step, level, and salary increases.

In the political setting, too, women mention becoming visible to cer-

tain male "gate keepers." Even a woman whose rise in volunteer politics was

entirely through a woman's organization, says:

> A man first got me interested in running . . . I had not
> wanted to run for office . . . This man belongs to an
> organization that picks candidates. He wrote me a nice
> letter telling me why I should run. It was a shock.

Her woman's organization friends offered their support, and she gradually began

to see herself as a possible candidate.

One hard working volunteer campaigner was asked to run for office

by the male party chairman because the political opponent was a woman and,

according to the informant, "some men turned pale at the mere mention" of the

idea of running against a woman. When she asked him, "Why me?"

> Well, you're a woman and this should be a woman's race.
> Besides, you're a good campaigner and we think you can
> win. (Priest, 1958: 134)

In this case her visibility came from hard work and effective campaigning for

others, but it also came from her sex. Being female increased her visibility

for this particular opportunity. In 1950 this was rare. Today it is not so rare

to achieve visibility for being female, in politics or in other settings, as the

following quotes testify:

I felt that I won because of the timeliness of being
female.

I think I got to the bench in the first instance as a
result of inverse discrimination.

It (being female) gives you visibility! (laughter)
There isn't any question about that! To that
extent it is an advantage, of course.

It came to my attention that there is a rivalry between military
bases and branches in pushing "their" women. When one woman's grade is
raised, the men in other bases begin the wheels rolling to see if they can't raise
"their" woman's grade. This must not be confused with a tendency to accept
more women into managerial positions. The existing woman managers at high
levels, of whom there are very few, are advanced like mascots at football games.
This is a very recent phenomenon. It bothers one of the women:

Every division is trying to get their women out front.
That's what I tell (her superior) when he tries to get me
to this dinner or that dinner. I say, "you are exploiting
me again!" (laughter) The humor has to be worked very
cleverly.

She prefers simpler times when recognition depended more on merit. She thinks
reverse discrimination causes resentment among subordinates, especially women
not selected for advancement. She is in the delicate position of humoring her
military bosses while trying to maintain the respect and loyalty of civilian
subordinates. Losing the respect and loyalty of either group will endanger her
future.

Visibility can be enhanced by personal uniqueness. In addition to being
female, itself unusual in high positions, the informants possessed a wide array of
unusual personal traits. Some decorated their offices with flamboyance or

displayed unexpected "female" objects such as cookbooks, a wig done up in rollers of paper money, or dolls. One about five feet tall, was unforgettable as she played the Jewish mother, hands on hips, scolding men nearly two feet taller. Another, close to six feet tall, wore a Marilyn Monroe style wig and huge false eyelashes which she batted at men much shorter than herself, while firmly and quietly giving them direction. Some of the ethnic women I observed prized their ethnicity. Accents had been carefully maintained, after decades of residence in the United States. One informant wore striking South American jewelry that covered her entire chest, though otherwise her taste appeared ordinary. Most of the women possessed loud voices and, by female standards, an unusually forceful style of speaking. I can think of other prominent women in the nation, not interviewed here, who cultivate personal uniqueness, appearing, for example, in unusual hats. Perhaps personal uniqueness plays some kind of role in their successful careers. This possibility was supported by the response of one informant with reference to her strikingly old-fashioned Madame Pompadour hairstyle.

> It's a trademark. When I walk down the street . . . even
> in the state, in airports, people will stop me and ask if
> I'm (X).

Sexual attractiveness may also increase visibility. One informant says being female can be an advantage, "especially if she's beautiful." But the visibility advantage can be offset by problems. This woman says a great deal of her rise in the organization was due to her boss falling in love with her, a circumstance which created the undying enmity of certain men. She quickly adds:

> You have to remember that when you get that high you
> can't be put into a position like that based on sex. That
> would flop the whole directorate. It's got to be ability.
> Everybody knows that. Even if you would go to bed with

your boss, he wouldn't put you in that position because
if you were not good at work, that would reflect on him.

This worry about a negative reflection on the male "gate keepers" may be a dis-

advantage to most women, at least while they are young. A different adminis-

trator says:

> . . . younger women are suspect as sex objects. Since
> almost all advancement has to be through men, men are
> very conscious of that. They will appear to be favoring
> a woman because of something in their relationship. As
> a woman gets older, that becomes much less of a factor.

In politics women may also receive special visibility if they are attractive. One

politician says before her first election opponents characterized her as a "dizzy

blonde." Immediately following the election, before she had a chance to prove

her capabilities, she received an inordinate amount of attention from the press.

Though this embarrassed her, the attention in itself was not a liability. There

may even be a positive effect of this attention. People seem to feel it is espe-

cially noteworthy if an attractive woman does a good job.

Of course many women with a "dizzy blonde" image would fail to get

elected in the first instance. Another politician says this is because

> The older you get, the more you look like Margaret Chase
> Smith, the more acceptable you become. For a man it's
> the other way around. (Pacific Sun (2-19-22, 1974,
> Dianne Feinstein, "The Woman Behind the Politician."
> p. 15)

In most settings, some amount of visibility for women is institution-

alized in the form of special awards for service. Most of my informants had

been the recipients of such awards. Mother of the Year, Outstanding Business

Woman, Woman of the Year in Business, Woman of Achievement (Business and

Professional Women's Clubs), mention in Who's Who of American Women, Award

66

of the Women Lawyers' Association, Angel of Distinction (Los Angeles business association), Woman of Tomorrow (Welfare Federation), Outstanding Civilian Woman (civil service), Woman of Achievement Award (Am. Fed. Soroptimist Clubs), and numerous awards given by newspapers and magazines for the outstanding 20 to 75 women in the country are some of the awards earned by women I interviewed. Such awards enhance visibility. However, awards open to both sexes are more coveted. There is a suspicion that open awards require higher standards. Besides the ambiguity about standards, the women who had earned open awards felt their visibility had been greatly enhanced because they had been selected from a much greater pool of contestants. Nevertheless, the presence of special awards for women has the effect of increasing the visibility of women in high positions.

In summary, both structural conditions and personal qualities contribute to visibility. In politics women have frequently developed a more demanding, but quite successful means of maintaining visibility.* The loose structure allows inventiveness. In the relatively more structured and slow-changing world of government bureaucracies, visibility for hard work and work attraction is

---

* There may be a physical limit to how much visibility a person can gain through "scut work" and "one-on-one" service to people. Lee (1974) finds that women politicians spend considerably more hours per month on political activities than their male counterparts. An assemblywoman, who brought the study to my attention, says she believes this explains why Werner (1968) found that women have been much more successful in their elective campaigns in relatively unpopulous states and districts. Lacking "normal" party support and financial backing, a woman still stands a chance of winning if she can personally meet a large proportion of constituents. The truly incredible amount of time spent by the representative of a very populous and urbanized district on political activities, especially in "responsiveness to the myriad frustrations and aggravations that beset the average citizen of her district" (Biography of Assemblywoman March Fong) means that she must get by with very little sleep -- usually four or five hours. Surely this would present a physical limit for most people.

institutionalized through regular inspections. But formal inspections of work load are not enough. Women in bureaucracies had to become visible as management potential. This usually meant coming to the attention of a superordinate man. The attention of key men was also an important factor in the beginnings of political careers. The presence of special awards for women provides visibility for women in high positions of all varieties. One informant mentions a further structural condition that may favor positive visibility.

> Lawyers easily evaluate whether other lawyers are
> getting out the work, and getting it our correctly . . .
> In other words you can't make a lot of wrong guesses
> and impress other lawyers.

This suggests that whenever people are evaluated by others who do similar work, there is less chance of arbitrary discrimination. This opinion does not coincide with Epstein's, who believes lack of access to male cliques inhibits the advancement of female professionals.

Unique personal qualities may increase the chances of recognition for one's work. Exactly how these factors are related to success is complex and requires further investigation. Being female in a top position increases visibility in itself, but, as with other personal qualities, the relationship with success is somewhat ambiguous. Several informants thought that at some point in their careers being female provided beneficial visibility.

THE BIG OPPORTUNITY

A big opportunity is one that, if taken, ushers a woman into a higher level of responsibility or into an organization with greater opportunities. In business it means taking advantage of a new marketing situation, in politics it usually means running for an office, and in government it means accepting a promotional or appointment opportunity. In civil service the opportunity often begins as an invitation by a superior to attend a school of management. In analyzing such opportunities, I will report both conditions for being offered the opportunity and conditions for accepting it.

Visibility and all the conditions that went into it, is unquestioningly the most important condition for being offered an opportunity that becomes a career turning point. On rare occasions does the administrator or party official have only one choice -- only one visible person -- to select for advancement. Two informants had this experience as an important point in their careers: they were the only people available to do the job. I will discuss these cases later in connection with conditions for accepting opportunities, for lately they have not. They are unusual for not accepting opportunities, and for not experiencing competition for their jobs. The other twelve informants experienced a great deal of competition for the positions they have held and hold.

The most important structural condition for a woman's receiving an opportunity for advancement is the lack of sexual barriers, formal or informal. Obviously there were no formal barriers in the setting investigated or these women would not be there. However, most surmounted informal barriers on their climb upward. One administrator mentions the kind of barrier discussed by Epstein. (1971, p. 169)

> . . . up to a certain point. You can make certain
> breakthroughs . . . Then you begin to reach artificial
> barriers. A great deal depends on who is in charge
> of the office. I remember in the (X) office there was a
> fear that if too many women achieved high positions,
> this would be discouraging to the men. So there was a

> kind of rationing. Sometimes this was expressed,
> sometimes not.

This particular woman was lucky. She was promoted before other qualified

women appeared on the scene and before a particular man reached a position

high enough to make a difference. Another competent woman who entered her

organization later was "held" for a long time.

> She got to the point where she didn't achieve recognition
> . . . My promotion, instead of triggering hers, worked
> in the reverse.

The man blocking her recognition "felt that women should <u>not</u> get into supervisory

positions. If you had interviewed him, he would have told you so."

> Women politicians also experience this kind of rationing.

> But I will say this: My being a (elected official) probably
> hurts other women's chances. I think men would say,
> "We already have one there. That's enough!"

Thus, being the first woman in a high position in an organization explains some

of the success of the women interviewed.

Several women in government bureaucracies were offered opportunities

under conditions of rapid expansion of the organization, or a sudden expansion of

responsibilities within the part of the organization in which they worked. Rapid

expansion of an organization causes a personnel panic. Qualified people are in

too short supply because the work is new. Under these circumstances one in-

formant assumed the duties of a branch manager when, officially, she was a

clerk typist. Later her position was upgraded to reflect her expanded duties.

Twenty-eight years later, after continuing growth of the organization, she is a

top manager of a very large operation. This is an extreme case of the effect of

rapid expansion on career advancement. In less extreme forms, organizational

expansion increased the opportunities of four other women working in bureaucracies.

Rapid expansion of the responsibilities within a woman's particular area within the organization increases the likelihood of recognition for efficient work and work attraction. When organizations have too many people for the work produced, there is less opportunity for work attraction and its resulting visibility. When there is an overload of work, a hard working, efficient woman can attract much work, thus becoming visible as an indispensable person in the department.

It is noticeable that most of the women interviewed are currently attempting to expand their work load in one way or another. In business, of course, expanding sales mean greater income. The political women were all especially interested in increasing the number of personal contacts with constituents. As mentioned above, this is not necessarily a typical activity of legislators. One informant holds a position formerly defined as narrowly administrative. She has transformed the position into a focal point of many intersecting community interests, drawing into her orbit community leaders from the wider Los Angeles area. She compares her activities with those of her various predecessors.

> Some have done nothing but just sit . . . That's not my
> bag. I happen to be a person who is involved, interested,
> and active . . . I have a whole lot of projects going this
> year.

A government administrator attributes some of her promotions to "wanting to push the organization beyond its present level." She contrasts her efforts to expand the organization's influence to the "content" attitude of most of her colleagues. She says "they were making good salaries." In other words, though she too made a good salary, she was not content with the influence of the

71

organization. She is responsible for increasing its responsibilities and influence, which in turn increases her workload.

Though most informants attribute their effort to increase their workload to personal traits -- to being "movers and shakers" -- it is tempting to conclude that they are aware that their chances for advancement increase when the workload increases. In other words, women have experienced success under conditions of expansion, and they therefore attempt to perpetuate those conditions. Perhaps if other means had been more successful, they would develop different strategies. In any case, expansion of the duties of the organization was an important structural condition for career advancement among the women interviewed.*

Informal barriers to female advancement in the form of unofficial "tests" administered by prejudiced men usually work against female opportunities. On the other hand, such unofficial tests can actually increase the opportunities of unusually personable and highly competent women. I have therefore included prejudice among structural conditions that have contributed to their career opportunities, though this factor must always be qualified.

Male prejudice was encountered by all informants. The expectation of certain men was that all women would be incompetent in managerial positions. In one case a woman's supervisor was a southern military man who said openly that women ought to be working for 25 cents an hour. She was a branch supervisor at the time. One of his good friends was a fellow supervisor. It became

---

* Hacket (1967) suggests that people in top positions expand the influence of their organizations because this is the principal means of advancement.

widely known that her superior was "out to get her" as he embarked on a program

of inspecting all the files in all the branches. He promised to fire any branch

chief whose files were not perfect. She says she has always been a perfectionist.

Therefore her files were perfect when he inspected them. The man was forced to

fire his good friend after finding chaos in those files. The incident triggered a

subsequent opportunity for her because it afforded her extraordinary visibility.

Another unofficial test was initiated by a woman seeking an

advancement.

> The man . . . interviewing was very honest. He said, "I
> do not believe in promoting women, and I don't believe
> women should be in supervisory positions." We had quite
> a discussion about why he believed that. (smile)

She convinced him that, whether or not she was capable, she would continue to

apply and make a nuisance of herself to him. Therefore, it would be to his bene-

fit to try her on a temporary basis for one year, and said:

> Any time you feel like bumping me back down, if you feel
> like it -- if you feel I'm not doing it right -- you can.

He accepted her condition. During the year he had no cause to "bump her back

down," and she "went right on from there." I asked her why he didn't simply

hire the man competing for the job.

> He wanted the man, and he didn't think I could do it.
> But I gave him the challenge. It was an opportunity for
> him to prove his point. He expected me to fail. Then
> he could say, "See, a woman can't do it." Dirty pool!
> (laughter) I told him, too, "If I can't do it, at least I
> want to prove it to myself. Then I'll sit down and
> behave myself (stop applying)."

Both these instances of unofficial tests in which women were expected

to fail were strictly contrary to civil service law, but neither woman complained to the Inspector General. I feel this reluctance to "rat on" superiors becomes known -- it also becomes part of their visibility as loyal, company women.

One woman elected by her peers experienced something like a special test for women. Prior to her election as assistant to the top administrator, uncontested elections were the rule.

> Formerly it was a matter of seniority -- automatic election of most senior member . . . By the time it became "my turn" as it were, we had contested elections both times.

She won the contested election for position as assistant, and the following one for top administrator. I asked her if being a woman had anything to do with the fact the elections were contested.

> I think so. Maybe if I had been a man I would have gone in and no one would have bothered to run against me. The person just before me had no opposition.

Winning a contested election carries more honor than being awarded a position on the basis of seniority; therefore, the "test" has enhanced her career opportunities.

Women politicians experience contested elections regularly. In this sense, elections are like the civil service inspections and the informal tests rolled up into one. Women politicians experience additional "tests."

> In my first years, here, some (male colleagues) delighted in baiting me or (another informant) . . . They loved dis- covering a mistake we made, so we had to work twice as hard as males to make sure we didn't make any.

She says this effort to be perfect has a positive consequence in the long run.

> Citizens . . . view women as a little more honest because the few of us who have been in office have been kind of showcase examples and we've worked very hard to prove ourselves.

In the sense that citizens are to politicians what ranking superiors are to civil servants -- in terms of promotions -- the results of the several tests are the same. The woman who "passes the test" becomes a showcase example, with increased visibility for her hard, effective work. In this sense, negative male attitudes have the consequence of contributing to career advancement, providing she passes the tests.

It goes without saying that the average woman -- and average man -- would not be able to surmount such barriers. These barriers constitute a continuing selection for the best talent. Because they are directed only at women, they select for higher levels of competence and integrity in women than in men.

The barrier of prejudice also selects for greater perserverance, strength of character, and commitment. Special "tests" are only the most obvious example of this selection. Consider the following:

> Being a woman is viewed negatively in this job, by some people. They might feel the same about me as a person, whether I was a man or a woman, but they say woman.

> How do you handle these people?

> I'm very tired now. I don't have much tolerance any more. I'm impatient. I don't worry a lot about that any more. I just go in. I don't have time for that.

A lesser woman might have quit. This one "just goes in." Surely this continuing process toughens the best and eliminates the weakest characters.

In summary, structural conditions that favor the advancement of these women included the lack of formal barriers, rapid expansion of the organization, working in an organization with no women in high positions, and perhaps even prejudice itself.

In addition to structural conditions that favored the advancement of the women interviewed, personal attitude played a role. Assuming that several visible candidates for a position are equally well qualified and no reverse discrimination exists, what quality will dispose a person to select a particular woman for a high position? A civil service administrator responds.

> I think (X) was looking for somebody who had more to give the organization, that had the organization at heart and wanted to push it beyond its present level.

This woman chastizes some young women liberationists who want to be promoted. She speaks of this attitude of "having the organization at heart."

> I'm going to look at you twice and ask myself, "Do you really represent the government? or are you really representing yourself -- your own way of doing things?" . . . I look at you and I wonder, "Should I send you to these schools? develop you? I think you've got some potential, but I don't think you've got the attitude."

An appointed administrator explains her attitude toward work.

> It means that you have a certain view of things, and that you proceed in a certain pattern. It's not working a given number of hours. If it takes 24 hours a day, then you have to do that. This is not a job, it is a mission. An awesome responsibility.

She attributes all her opportunities to "gravitating" toward unique people who also gravitated toward her.

The owner-manager of a world-wide corporation uses similar imagery. I asked her, "What is the most important factor in selecting top managers?"

> The ideal situation is to hire someone who you relate to -- the chemistry is right -- and who is highly skilled in the work . . . In earlier years if the chemistry wasn't right, I wouldn't hire them. In more recent years I've

hired them for their specialization and not worried
about the chemistry. I think it's been a mistake.

Her corporation has lost some ground in recent years. She looks back with

pleasure on the years when she and her top managers worked together as a team,

having fun, conquering the business world with identical philosophies and close

"chemistry."

The closeness between a well-liked elected official and her constit-

uents may be of the same nature.

I go in. I feel at home . . . In the black areas . . .
there's a repartee, a warmth. This is a natural
constituency to me. The same in Chinese and Latino
groups. Those are my bases.

Voters do not exactly "offer opportunities" to people to run. There is a mutual

reaching out, a gravitating toward each other, a chemistry that in the final

analysis is responsible for the woman attaining her position.

If these opinions can be summarized in sociological language, they

probably express Homan's meaning when he said that a leader is one who comes

closest to realizing the norms the group values highest. In this case, these

women felt they attained high positions -- partly because their devotion to certain

critical causes was perceived by people in positions to advance or elect them.

Now they use that criteria, or feel they should use it, in selecting others for

leadership positions. It is possible that, while loyalty is an important requirement for all career advancement, women may place even more importance upon it than men.*

Accepting the Big Opportunity

Conditions for accepting opportunities are of two types: (1) positive reaction of husband and family, and (2) positive personal feelings, in that order. The most important consideration that determines whether the informants will accept a big opportunity is whether their husbands would agree to move, should the advancement require it.

> He didn't really want me to run. He's a little threatened by it . . . I think he realized he can't turn me into a homebody, but he would prefer it if I were . . . That's why I say that I will stay here (in this job). I am fortunate that the Legislature is here. I could do that, and still be in Sacramento.

The elected official quoted above is unique in being the only informant whose husband is "threatened" by her position. She answered a flat "no" to the possibility of his moving elsewhere for the sake of her career.**

The following are representative responses to questions about how husbands felt when or if a wife's promotion meant moving to a new location:

> My husband was always happy when I brought home a lot of money. (He relocated on her behalf.)

---

* Hacket discusses the way in which the concept "merit" is often imbued with the idea of loyalty as a promotional requirement in civil service organizations. ". . . the testing of loyalties (is) a continuous feature of organizational life." (p. 64) Constantini and Craik (1972) find that "women leaders (of party organizations) grant significantly greater importance than the male leaders to 'strong party loyalty' as a reason for initially becoming involved in politics." Additionally, women pursue more party activities that "demonstrate . . . loyalty to state party leadership." (Ibid.) In contrast, the authors found male party leaders to be more self-serving.

** At the time of printing, this couple is divorced.

He beamed with quiet pride (while I was running). (He)
would lead the applause when I had finished speaking
and went around shaking hands. (Priest, 19□□:84)

His work is such that he doesn't have to punch a time
clock. He can organize his business and be free to
spend time with me.

My husband is in a position where he can retire. With
his interests in art and music, he can have just as much
fun there (Washington) as here. We're free for the first
time in many years.

My husband said, "You must do it. California needs it."
(He lives and works in a different city.)

Two informants had been divorced before the interview, partly be-

cause of tensions arising from their jobs. Now they are married to men who are

"supporters." The husbands' positive attitude is highly valued by all married

informants, and many of them dwell on it.

My husband wanted me to do it. He was perfectly sure I
could. He is fantastic.

He is my best supporter . . . I consulted him and the whole
family before I ran for office, because I knew it was going
to change their lives . . . They were willing. They felt it
might be exciting, might be a challenge.

He's a special man, secure in himself, as he has to be
married to someone with my lifestyle.

Yes, he is an unusual man. There aren't very many men
who would let their wives take the front position with the
outside world . . . It takes a very big man. He has less
hangups than most men.

I happen to be lucky; I have a husband who truly enjoys
seeing me do these things. He's secure in his own pro-
fession; I'm not a threat.

The positive attitudes of these husbands affected their wives' decisions to take

opportunities.

In two cases husbands openly acknowledge the greater importance of the wife's career. The men's careers are considered of lower priority should conflict arise. In three cases husband and wife carry on simultaneous careers in different cities, commuting irregularly to see each other. The remaining four married women live and work in the same city with their husband, and his career is considered by the two of them to be at least equal in importance to hers.

THE LATERAL TRANSFER

Career, as used here, may begin with any work in any organization, whether paid or unpaid. Four informants traveled far in unpaid spirals prior to their appointments or elections in present leadership positions. One progressed to statewide president of the League of Women Voters. A second became president or other top position in numerous community social and cultural volunteer organizations. A third volunteered work for various education and welfare community projects, later becoming a member of two statewide commissions. The fourth worked her way from block-precinct worker to national committeewoman and co-chairman (sic) of a successful presidential candidate's campaign.

These women transferred from the top level of each of these organizations into related but different and larger organizations. Informants who began working for salaries experienced such transfers. Occupying the top rung of any spiral makes a woman visible to those who are in positions to offer opportunities from their related spirals. This is due to contacts she makes in the course of her job.

It is often thought that women doom themselves to middle management when they enter small organizations, or that women are wasting their energies in volunteer or women's organizations. But these fourteen women's careers show that lateraling is not only common, but also expected.

The following quote suggests the existence of a norm for lateraling from the tops of spirals.

> Traditionally there aren't a tremendous lot of opportunities from this job, but there are some.

One of the traditional opportunities from her job is going into business. She would "find it intriguing" to go into business, but she fears sex barriers would prevent her from retaining her present salary after transfering. Men before her have not had that problem. However, she has a better educational background than they, and she now bides her time until a truly attractive offer comes from her many contacts in the business world.

One of the top civil servant informants similarly waits for an opportunity from the business or political world, with which she has considerable contact.

Two important personal conditions for lateraling are (1) ambition to rise in influence, and (2) willingness to continue working hard. Two important structural conditions are (1) whether that spiral offers favorable conditions for advancement, and (2) whether it involves a geographic move. The lateral transfer, therefore, is the equivalent of an opportunity within an organization, with all of its attendant, value-added conditions.

If conditions are right and the woman has come to the end of her monetary and influence ambitions, what happens? Where do spirals end? Perhaps my data provide a possible answer.

Two women I spoke to on the telephone but did not tape an interview (they are refusing interviews), appeared to have eased off the top rung of their spirals. They no longer work hard in the organization, though they are on salary and maintain beautiful offices in the executive suites. They are no longer interested in work-related visibility. They are extremely active in cultural activities which afford them great recognition there. One of my informants is in the process of easing off the top of her work spiral. She says she has just "formalized" a one-third week, and is now more a consultant to her corporation. Her considerable energies are now spent in making a movie with her writer-son. One political informant no longer interested in career advancement is pleased to have highways and lakes named after her. Much of her energy is now spent carrying legislation for the creation of historical museums and landmarks.

If these events can be interpreted in the spiral scheme, perhaps they indicate a lateral transfer from the world of work into the cultural world of meaning and history.

CONCLUSION

I cannot conclude, with Fogarty (1971), that chance or accident plays an unusually large role in the careers of women in top jobs. The few women he studied in Britain had experienced some fortuitous opportunities in their careers, as some of my fourteen informants had. But luck plays a role in men's careers, too.

The important differences between men and women in achieving leadership positions lies in the processes of their careers. Women believe they have worked harder, achieved more, overcome more barriers, while being

Chart II

Review of Conditions Affecting
CAREER SPIRALS

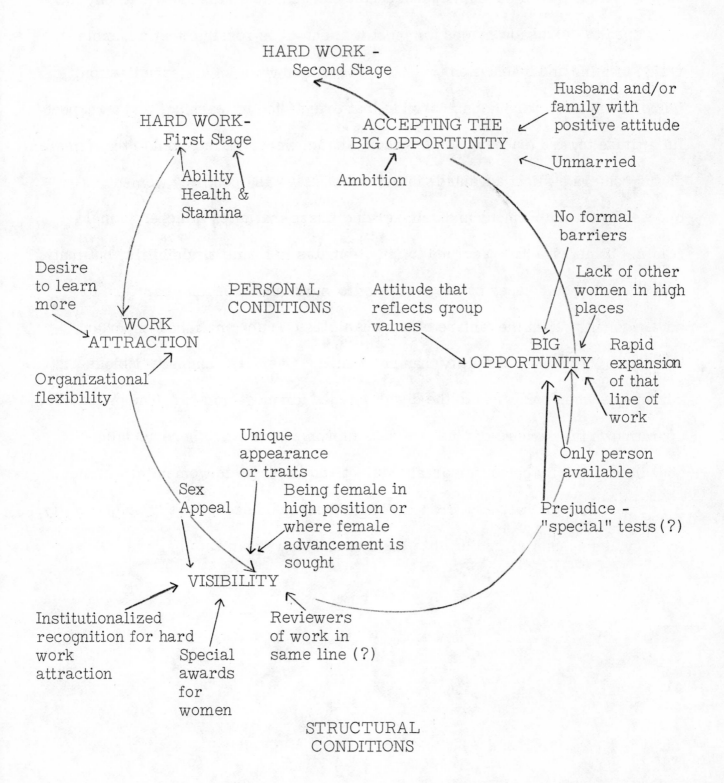

HARD WORK -
Second Stage

HARD WORK-
First Stage

Ability
Health &
Stamina

ACCEPTING THE
BIG OPPORTUNITY

Ambition

Husband and/or
family with
positive attitude

Unmarried

Desire
to learn
more

PERSONAL
CONDITIONS

Attitude that
reflects group
values

No formal
barriers

WORK
ATTRACTION

Lack of other
women in high
places

Organizational
flexibility

BIG
OPPORTUNITY

Rapid
expansion
of that
line of
work

Unique
appearance
or traits

Only person
available

Sex
Appeal

Being female in
high position or
where female
advancement is
sought

Prejudice -
"special" tests (?)

VISIBILITY

Institutionalized
recognition for hard
work
attraction

Special
awards
for
women

Reviewers
of work in
same line (?)

STRUCTURAL
CONDITIONS

offered fewer opportunities, and were able to accept fewer opportunities. When they have done all these things, one cannot say they got to the top by accident.

The advantages they had because of female status are relatively few compared to the disadvantages for most women. It is possible that a humble frame of mind and orientation to detail, associated with female socialization, helped them work hard. It is possible that orientation to learning, and a respectful attitude toward teachers, helped them attract work. It is possible that female status confers a slight advantage in being perceived as "company women" as opposed to the autonomous and self-serving image that often attaches to male status. Some advantage accrued to female status in terms of visibility, but that was offset in some cases by the necessity to surmount unofficial barriers to advancement. Then the fanfare of a woman's having accomplished important work gave them more visibility than some men. Overall, these are dubious advantages when compared to the disadvantages for most women. The processes, operating in the careers of these successful women (analyzed here as value-added), continually select for greater talent and integrity in women than in men. It is small wonder that, as a group, I found them to be exceptionally bright, witty, friendly, enthusiastic, and loyal to their causes and organizations.

Chapter III

THE FEMININE LEAD

In this chapter I will address myself primarily to the questions: What are woman leaders like? How are they different from each other? How are they similar? What strategies appear to work best for them?

The problem of finding the most appropriate criterion by which to differentiate these fourteen woman leaders was not simple. It is tempting to say they are all different and leave it at that. But the task here is to focus on the way in which feminine status conflicts or blends with leadership status.

Looking at the data in this way, it became obvious that the women relate to their jobs, broadly speaking, in two ways. Some employ traditionally female kinds of interaction. Others do not. In other words, some attempt to blend traditional female roles with leadership status. I call this Type I style. Type II leaders emulate "male" leadership styles, disavowing female kinds of interaction on the job. These two types are not totally mutually exclusive. There was some shifting between types. Two women displayed elements of both styles, and one was particularly difficult to characterize in either way. Again, typologies are only useful devices. I do not mean to imply, furthermore, that this cleavage is the only way the informants' styles can be viewed.

TYPE I STYLE: PLAYING MAMA

The following selections suggest that some women consciously play a motherly role.

> I have always had a way of dealing with things. It
> revolves around the fact that I did not grow up to be

a professional. I act . . . as I have always acted: a
mother, a citizen, a lady, a concerned person . . .

Notice that she cites "mother" first among her other roles, then "lady." I asked

her if being female gave her any advantages in leadership.

I don't know if this is for good or ill, or whether it is
for other women, but for me, I think the fact that I am
a woman -- there's a sort of Jewish mother syndrome.
They accept it (direction) because of the way I tell them.
It's like, "Children, we have to do that -- right now."
(laughter) It's as if I really love them and I'm going to
push them.

This was my first interview. I was surprised to encounter motherli-

ness in the next interview with a Protestant woman. It surfaced early in the

interview, without any prompting on my part.

What experience was most helpful in preparing you for this
position?

Being a mother is the best experience in supervising people.
I try to be a good mother in this Division. I rule by faith in
people's ability, not by fear.

I began asking women if they took a motherly role in their job.

A lot of young folks relate to me in a motherly way now.
I find young folks coming to me and seeming to need
something from me. Personal advice, personal help,
personal strength giving.

Did they do this when you were younger?

Yes, they did it. I think it's more the person, or the
chemistry . . . rather than the age. My sister was
like that. Everybody came to her, and I think I've sort
of taken on the role she used to have.

Some informants blur the line between relating to children and to

people at work, though they are less explicit in playing a motherly role. A law-

maker discusses it:

They (men) are short with people. I think when you have
children you develop understanding. All these things
happen with kids -- a mother listens and pays attention
and has feelings . . . I have more patience and identification with problems.

One administrator felt a specifically <u>motherly</u> role can be unfavorable

in leadership because "older women sometimes become set in their ways." She

does, however, consciously adopt a traditionally feminine leadership role. She

relates a conversation with a male subordinate:

He said, "You teach everybody you meet, unconsciously or
consciously." What I try to do is to get everybody to their
ability . . . He told me, "You know, you're tenacious.
You've not only done this for me, and I appreciate it, but
(X) -- who had so little when he came in -- you've developed
him into one of the best (. . .) we have. I don't think you
even realize the adulation we have for you . . ." I was
thinking about this afterwards, and I think it (teaching) has
helped make me become successful.

Her style of interaction is very similar to that of women who play a

mother role. She believes women have unique abilities. She aims to "develop

people," to use empathy and informality; she uses special strategies to "relax"

prejudiced people. Relationships are of primary importance to her -- as a way

of achieving high production -- and she relates to people in what she feels is a

typically "feminine way." Importantly, she links her managerial abilities with

motherly behavior.

<u>What advantages are there in being a woman?</u>

I think the greatest advantage a woman has is that she has
a greater ability to <u>sense</u> how other people feel . . . The
ESP, or the sensitivity that a woman has . . . That's more
a woman's ability than a man's.

<u>That's an advantage?</u>

A definite advantage. Mothers have this with children.
. . . I think this is something men <u>may</u> have, but have
never developed.

At a different point in the interview she referred to a difficult man -- one who

would not resign under pressure -- as a "mama's boy."

Altogether, seven -- fully half of the fourteen informants -- either

say openly they play a mother role or relate to people in a motherly or teacherly

way.

Type I women reported few incidents in which people rejected them on

account of being female. They <u>want</u> to be regarded as female. They frequently

mention their female status in jokes around the office or in meetings. Men and

women, young and old, relate to them as a <u>female</u> superior. People appear to be

comfortable, and there appears to be unqualified acceptance or respect for the

woman in charge. In only one instance did an informant mention management

problems related to Type I leadership.

<u>Does having a motherly relationship to people give you</u>
<u>an advantage in a leadership position?</u>

Yes, it does -- most people were relatively easy for me to
lead. I was -- a strong leader. If I had a flaw in leadership,
it was that I got very involved in what I was leading.

<u>You had almost a family kind of empathy?</u>

Yes, and I work <u>with</u> them and get involved with their
problems, instead of saying "report to me." I would get
in it with them. (pause) That's fine for a small business,
but when you get up into big business, then comes the
question of how you delegate that to somebody and make
that person responsible and make him carry the thing.

She says the ability to delegate without abdicating responsibility is difficult for a

person with her style of leadership.

The appropriate way (from the books) is to have a plan and then be measured against the plan in a cold, dispassionate way. That, I think, is a male skill . . . I've been trying to learn it. (laughter) I think I've learned it, but . . . (pause) I don't particularly like that kind of technique of operating. I'm not comfortable in that kind of setting. I'm happier being involved. (pause) I know now, after 30 years, that I prefer a smaller operation. (laughter) It's more fun. And that's what it's all about. Where's the fun?

Pressures Toward Mothering -- Birth of a Role

A role means that expectations about appropriate behavior emanate from both actor and others. The mother role apparently emanates partly from coworkers.

Do people relate to you as a woman?

Probably, you're right. Other women, and perhaps some of the younger boys. I try to be very friendly and I have a great sympathy for the younger generation.

Do they comment about this?

Well, the ones that I work with at the office call me "mother." (laughter)

How do you feel about that?

I laugh about it -- I think it's great. One of the young men, who was a trainee, is now in a high level job in Washington, D. C., was the first one. When he left, he would write to me and sign the letters "Number 3 Son."

She says this has "caught on" now, and she likes it. It helps her "assert" herself in a "friendly way."

A woman in a different setting says she has always noticed men wanting to relate to her as if she were a mother figure, even when she was young.

89

<u>Do only young people relate to you as a mother?</u>

Differing ages. For example a man older than I, who had
quit a year before, wanted me to get him his job back. I
did it. He was so happy! He <u>had</u> to talk to me. He was
like a little boy, and I was like his mother. That was the
most marked among the men.

<u>Do you welcome this mother role, or wish it wasn't there?</u>

In that case I wished it wasn't there, because I knew the
brilliance in that mind. But I welcome it in anybody else.
I usually enjoy people's relating to me as a mother because
I feel it is a sign they have confidence in me.

Sometimes the suggestion toward mothering emanates first from equal status

colleagues.

In the campaign I was the "den mother." I was the only
woman on the ticket, don't you remember them calling me
that? (laughter) I rather liked it!

Since the successful campaign, others have applied that label to her. The fact

that she likes it and reminds people about it probably helps explain its popularity.

In one instance an informant felt pressures toward mothering, but

rejected the role. She prefers Type II leadership.

<u>Are you conscious of any role you play?</u>

(long pause) It really makes me provoked when people --
my interns -- accuse me of having the mother instinct.
(pause) I really resent it.

<u>They must think you have a mother instinct.</u>

Yes, in dealing with some of the young people -- some of
them -- they'll make the remark, "Oh, that's the motherly
instinct."

<u>That irritates you?</u>

That irritates me.

<u>Why?</u>

(pause) I figure that if you are working, competing with men on a job, or if you're working in the same atmosphere and same conditions, and you're the only female -- I don't think anybody should show any special consideration.

She dislikes the attention to her sex which "mother instinct" brings. Perhaps, not coincidentally, this particular woman says she identifies with her father.

The pattern appears to be: A woman attains a leadership position. If she has not already established this mothering style during her spiral to the top, she now finds herself in a fairly normless position. Hints and small urgings from others suggest she adopt the mothering style. Often a predisposition exists for her to emulate her own mother or other female relative. She and her co-workers come to a mutual understanding that mothering or teaching (a less emotionally charged "female" role) is an appropriate role style for her. Now she finds it easier to assert herself in a friendly way.

Advantages of Playing Mama

All authority must be regarded as legitimate in the eyes of followers or it is not effective. For maximum effectiveness there must be a feeling of emotional acceptance of leadership. The woman on top may have a reputation of being the best, most effective, most loyal person available for the job. Additionally, she holds an office with authority. But at the tops of career spirals there may linger a suspicion that women are not the most appropriate leaders despite qualifications. Something more is needed. I suggest this need partly explains the flowering of mothering and teaching ideologies in female leadership. Mother and teacher are both legitimate female superordinate roles which have touched the lives of virtually every person in our society. It should not be surprising if, faced with a need to bolster their authority, women would turn to behavior patterns in which women traditionally play a dominant role. That this interaction style would add an extra dimension to authority, or unlock a latent authority status possessed potentially by all women, is suggested by one informant. The daughter of a strong, ethnic mother speaks about her success in directing and doing business with men.

> I still think men -- the older men, not the modern men -- still are very submissive to women in a way. The mother remembrances . . . It can work as a source of authority.

I had made a field note to myself about the easy way in which this woman gave direction to a distinguished looking, high level male subordinate who was older than herself, fondly calling him "Father." Her opinion that older men tend to be submissive to women -- her expectation that they will be submissive partly explains the ease of their relationship.

It may be paradoxical that so many of the women I interviewed feel they benefit from sexual type-casting as mothers that, apparently, is a disadvantage to most women. Symbolic interactive principles may go a long way toward explaining this apparent contradiction. Undoubtedly a woman who presents herself to men in a way that suggests she expects them to be submissive -- to have "mother remembrances" -- controls the situation better than a woman who thinks men have little respect for women. This may be so regardless of the upbringing of the men in question, though testing of this proposition must await a different kind of study. In any case, the "Mamas" I observed and talked to claim most people were easy for them to lead.

Do people respond to a "Mama" leader in any particular way? Are they "process" rather than "product" oriented? Does efficiency suffer, as

Stogdill's (1974) exhaustive review suggests? Type I leaders sometimes report

outright adulation of themselves, as in an earlier quote, "I don't think you even

realize the adulation we have for you." There is a tendency, sometimes

reported, for a "following" to develop among subordinates. An administrator

showed me a large leather swivel chair personally engraved with her name which

had been given to her by subordinates in a former position. Speaking of the

effectiveness of her style of leadership she says,

> It is the same here. I have the most marvelous coopera-
> tion!" . . . They are the same . . . people who have been
> working here all along, under different administrations.
> And yet the tremendous record that we have piled up has
> not been equaled in any state (or previous administration).
> My value was in being able to open the door, to permit
> them to do the job they were always capable of.

Another speaks to the effectiveness of getting personally involved in the problems

of subordinates.

> When you give them this undivided attention (she had
> helped a young woman in a difficult personal situation),
> they don't forget it. They develop a loyalty to the
> organization. Once they know I'm there to help them
> and guide them, then they will accept whatever guidance
> I give them.

Type I informants cite high productivity as a definite advantage of

that style of leadership. It is outside the scope of this study to compare produc-

tivity under different styles of leadership. Nonetheless, one observation is in

order. Stogdill's "person-oriented," Fiedler's "relationship-oriented,"

McGregor's "Theory Y" leadership -- roughly the same concepts -- have involved

a situational factor unmentioned by any of these authors. Nearly all their leaders

were men who lead, primarily, other men. When the leader is a woman and key

subordinates are men, we have a different situation, one that may make a critical difference when leadership styles are compared by productivity. We simply have no idea how productivity is affected by _female_ person-oriented leadership. The women who use this style claim it is very effective. Furthermore, I think we can make the assumption that, given the typically high standards for excellence and production, often imposed by outside critics, reality probably coincides with the perceptions of these leaders that their operations are highly productive.

There are other advantages in Type I leadership. A woman leader who displays her femininity openly has less to cover. She can spend her precious time on more important things. I observed one such woman openly forgetful on irrelevant details, like where she put her cigarettes. A male colleague called her "scatterbrained female" during a meeting. She laughed with the entire committee. One of her secretaries quickly sketched the cartoon on page 95 when I asked her what the boss was like. The overhead question mark refers to this "scatterbrainedness", used by this woman almost as a mark of distinction. The cartoon was xeroxed and mailed to me under her direction, illustrating her unconcerned acceptance of this stereotypical "female" trait. The same woman sometimes uses "female" analogies to make points, as did other "Mamas." The following quote also shows she _is_ concerned about important details.

> I'm the kind of detail person that says, "this is the goal you want to accomplish," and I look to see what kinds of things I have to do to get there. It's like a recipe.

Early in my observation I was surprised to see women in top positions putting on lipstick in public. I had thought this would have drawn unwanted attention to their sex. Two Type I leaders did it, not attempting to turn away or rush. One sat on a televised panel at the time. This lack of concern over appearances extends

94

beyond "female" things, I learned. I watched one "Mama" wipe her nose on a napkin and pick her teeth with a fork while sitting at the head table at a formal dinner attended by about three hundred prominent people, including press. One must remember that by "traditionally feminine" behavior in the context of Type I leadership, I do not necessarily include idealized "lady-like" behavior, but instead emphasize a motherly or teacherly style of interacting with subordinates and colleagues. I also do not mean to imply that these leaders were rude. It is a refreshing lack of pretense of all sorts that was noticeable among these women.

Type I women sing in the halls and clasp hands a fraction longer than one expects. They hug and pat people from janitors to superiors (and me!). They show emotion. Two reported crying on occasion. They are apt to be volatile in showing anger, but recover quickly. Interestingly, this type never reported being left out of male cliques or male activities. In this connection, one says she is not viewed as a threat to men.

> I don't seem to threaten in the sense that they (equal status colleagues) don't consider me a competitor. It's because I'm a woman I'm not seen as a competitor.

Perhaps the open demonstration of femaleness confer this important advantage. One aspect of traditional "femaleness" not demonstrated by informants of any type was coyness or flirtatiousness. Most informants talked about the importance and ease with which they "let me know where they stand." A younger informant says,

> I don't play around. But I'm a friendly person, and I like to go out to dinner and have drinks with people, etc. I'm just not going to get involved. When you get that reputation established, it's a lot easier to deal with men on the level on which I deal with men -- I deal mainly with men.

> The word gets around. You let them know right off the
> bat that you're not about to. You can establish that
> quite readily.

Another informant says even when she was younger men never "came on sexually"

when she was trying to conduct business. "I would think anybody past the age of

eighteen would know how to handle that. It just doesn't happen." The importance

of letting men know where they stand is explained by another woman.

> You got to let a guy know. Then once he <u>knows,</u> probably
> he feels more at ease because he feels, "OK, I don't have
> to make the pass that she's expecting," or "even though
> I'd like to, I'm not going to because she's not going to be
> susceptible.

There are other aspects of "traditionally female" which must not be

read into Type I style. Some popular literature has stressed the servile, self-

effacing, self-sacrificing nature of the mother role. This connotation was

practically absent from informants' conceptions, unless one takes the view that

developing an equal status atmosphere with subordinates is "self-effacing." They

typically spoke of doing "service" to others or to a cause, taking the view that

"developing people's potentials" or "helping people do what they do best" serves

the organization. It should be remembered that what serves the organization

serves its leaders.

Sloppiness or inefficiency are not tolerated by "Mamas" or any other

leader I interviewed. Type I leaders typically say they impose very high work

standards upon their subordinates and business associates, but these standards

are not quite as high as their personal standards, which they often view as un-

realistic for other people. Regarding the productivity of subordinates, one says,

"I'm pushy, I'm very tough. I mean it shall happen -- it shall happen!" While a different informant's male colleague waited to reach a delinquent business contact on a phone within earshot of the two of us, he told me, "You should here (her) talk to them. She really chews them out." "I chew," the woman repeated without pausing or looking up from her desk work.

Humor, used extensively by Type I women, serves definite purposes, especially, they say, the release of tension during meetings or conflicts. Bodily contact appears to relax people, an objective often mentioned by these leaders as an important aspect of their style. But bodily contact is neither sexual, weak, nor mushy. It is perhaps the most motherly aspect of this style.

Most "Mamas" describe the development of mothering techniques in connection with their present positions. Either they kept these tendencies somewhat under wraps during their earlier years or their lower level positions were not of a nature to call forth the role. Only one of the seven who I have included in Type I mentioned motherliness in connection with her career advancement.

> He liked my strength, and I heard from (his peers) that
> he liked my stability. (pause) I'm sure I was a mother
> image to him, even though he was my boss.

Being a mother-image to one's boss must be tricky -- perhaps an improbable role combination for most women. Another informant said women have to "watch it" (motherliness) in lower level positions, especially "when the woman is over-qualified for the job and when a young man -- her superior -- is stern." In her organization such a "stern" young man complained about an older woman under him calling him a "whipper-snapper" during a clash between them. The informant was called in to help settle the dispute. She felt this was an example of the mother-instinct poorly used, ultimately hurting the woman's chances for advancement.

Comparing "Mamas" by organizational type, I find more in large bureaucracies than in politics. There is a tendency for them to have less formal education, though one Mama was a college graduate. One should remember that this kind of factor analysis is unreliable, due to the small sample size.

TYPE II STYLE: ONE OF THE MEN

The four women who consciously put aside traditionally female ways of relating to people contrast sharply with Type I leaders. They are comfortable in more formal atmospheres. They appear to be less outspoken, refer to more people by their last names, or titles, and confine their interaction more to their peers. Whereas Type I leaders pride themselves on having very friendly relation-ships with subordinates, a Type II leader typically does not.

You don't develop close relationships with people under you?

No. Well, you can't put it that way. It all depends. I don't . . . like any other executive, I tend to go out with people -- there is a certain status group.

Your peers?

Yes. I don't go to the secretaries' room for coffee. I never have. I did for a little while as a (lower level manager). I discovered that the women secretaries really didn't like it. I stopped doing it.

In contrast, Type I women like to chat with subordinates; they feel comfortable having coffee and lunch with secretaries and subordinates when there is time. Apparently secretaries feel comfortable having coffee with them. Where-as the Type I leader tends to ignore -- even dissolve -- formal heirarchial relations as a means of increasing production, Type II women find the traditional status distances useful to them in conducting their business.

The following are examples of answers to the question of whether they play a mother role -- or whether others cast them in that role:

> No. Period. No jokes about it. I think they wouldn't dare! . . . I don't want them to see me as mother . . . They don't come to me with their problems.

> Is there a difference between motherly and fatherly? I'm certain that there is a parental feeling, but I don't think little <u>kids</u> respond to me as a mother, although I get along with many children extremely well.

Type II leaders stress a no-nonsense business atmosphere at work. A politician says, "No . . . when you walk into this room it's all business."

> <u>Do you ask them about their homelife?</u>

> No. Never. There are exceptions (when we go to a periodic office luncheon), but I don't like anybody to come in and say, "I like your hair-do" when we meet for a briefing in the morning -- any more than I would say that in that situation to somebody. Just as they would come in to speak with a man in the office, that's not going to be the opening comment.

I asked an administrator if she tries to develop a casualness. She answered bluntly, "No."

> <u>Do people call you by your first name?</u>

> My peers. I wouldn't like secretaries calling me by my first name. Nor do I ordinarily call them by first name.

In contrast, Type I leaders make it a point to use first names and ask about the homelife of subordinates. I was present when the opening comment of a subordinate to a Type I leader was, "I like your new hair-do!" She appeared to be pleased with the compliment.

The above quote typifies Type II leaders in that they often refer back to what they feel would be appropriate behavior for men in their positions. Because they consciously employ what they perceive as male standards of behavior, I have thought of them as "One of the Men." This is not to imply that all male leaders employ this style.

I asked whether they employed special strategies to gain the support of recalcitrant people. Type II leaders were either tonguetied from never having thought about such a thing, or they responded as one did, "No, I haven't. And I'm not sure you should."

In contrast, Type I leaders reported using such strategies, most of which were designed to "relax people" or establish better rapport. One Type I leader goes to the trouble of giving certain men extra choices of work rather than directives, so they will not feel they are being bossed by a woman. A Type II leader says she would tell a man who could not take direction to "shape up or ship out."

Type II leaders are less likely to look for personal rapport in hiring and firing.

> I do not look for that. This is a place where I probably
> am wrong. In fact I put on people who the rest of the
> staff -- they come in and tell me "he wants to be director"
> (get her job). He's driving everybody crazy. But I may
> tend to lean the other way. I do not look for somebody who
> has a good relationship with me. (She looks only for
> competence.)

Hiring or assigning jobs by rapport was a continuing theme among Type I leaders.

One Type II leader had been appointed largely because she managed to reduce the conflict rife in a Board that sets policy for her operation. Her

male predecessor had been "irascible" in his dealings with elected officials.
Remembering how Type I leaders felt a woman's presence in a tense meeting is
a softening influence, I asked her opinion.

> I suppose the answer one gives to that is "yes." But I
> don't really think so. I think that being a lawyer helps;
> it's the discipline.

She disavows sex status as an explanation. Female status is a common explanation for various successes among Type I leaders.

STATUS STRAIN: ORPHAN ANNIE

The potential conflict between female and leadership roles was,
obviously, largely overcome by most of the women I interviewed, though they
spoke of certain ambiguities. Type I leaders in particular appeared to operate
within a comfortable system of shared expectations for behavior. Type II women
also appeared comfortable acting as "task-oriented" leaders. (Fiedler, 1971)
Two women apparently experience considerable status conflict. Interviews,
observation, and remarks of others support this interpretation. Their voices
are not forceful. They do not lean forward across desks and tables in the confi-
dent way that Types I and II leaders do. A newspaper report about one of them
quoted a colleague saying, "you don't know exactly what she is thinking."

This woman acknowledged, in the interview, that men sometimes
misunderstood her. I asked whether men had attempted to "come on" sexually
when she wanted to conduct business. "Yes."

How do you handle that?

> I guide them to where I want them to behave. (pause)
> Usually it's the other way around. I wanted the relation-
> ship to be a date and it turned out to be business, and I
> was disappointed.

This was the only respondant who had experienced misunderstandings in the sexual area. Apparently the other leaders were more skillful in conveying their feelings to men, men were less able to manipulate them, or (one must admit of this possibility) these women were more honest in reporting. In any case, the strain of playing the feminine and leadership roles simultaneously apparently creates more confusion in this particular woman's interpersonal relations.

The two women in question attempt to emulate a "male" style of interaction. They want to be Type II leaders because they feel that this kind of leadership is appropriate in the worlds of business and politics. They verbally deny playing any female roles, yet their style of presenting themselves is unobtrusive and vulnerable -- classically feminine. For this reason I dubbed them Orphan Annies. I observed them waiting for men to open doors. They did not open doors for me, as both Types I and II had done. Subordinates probably sense the same vulnerability, unobtrusiveness, and hesitancy in interacting with them as I did. In America these traits are part of the female role, but not the leadership role.

In spite of their often repeated desire to be treated "same as a man," Orphan Annies sometimes unwittingly behave in a motherly fashion, though not forcefully enough to establish a mother-authority style. I think the following nicely exemplifies this uneasy mixture. Some high level men had challenged the woman's authority to set their pay.

> They were rude. They acted like five-year-olds. Bratty kids.

> And you were like the mother that said "no"?

>   Yes. (vigorous nod, then quickly) But then, a male
>   would probably be seen as a parent figure in the
>   same situation.

She had stressed earlier that being cast in a mother role irritated her. Yet she

conceptualizes this pay confrontation as a mother-child form of interaction.

When this was pointed out she quickly refers to how a man would act.

>   An elected "Orphan Annie" complains about the lack of service, com-

paring her situation with male colleagues.

>   . . . they (staff) have respect for me. But I don't get
>   the same service (as a man would). I think they uncon-
>   sciously expect me to do things that women ordinarily do.
>   For instance, they would hand me the thread and expect
>   me to sew on my own button. (pause) Also they fre-
>   quently hand me a telephone number and expect me to
>   call it. This is <u>unconscious</u>.

I asked her if she delegated most things. She answered, "I tend to do them

myself." She does these menial things, slightly resenting it. This may explain

why this woman is among the hardest workers. Though it may not sound as if

she has much influence, she does. It is very obvious from her success in cam-

paigning and the extent of her legislative successes that she, in fact, does delegate

much important work. The point is that she is bothered by her inability to dele-

gate more, especially the menial things. Type I and II leaders do not harbor

resentful feelings. A "Mama" would probably say, "What? You think I have all

day to spend on this junk (or other expletive)?" A Type II leader would quietly

and firmly delegate. Status conflict appears to prevent or limit this woman's

ability to make administering more satisfying.

>   There are other indications of strain. Men feel the need to apologize

to "Orphans" for using strong language. Sometimes these women feel resentful when male colleagues do not invite them to lunch. They say they sometimes feel left out of the male clique that predominates. Such problems are well documented by Epstein (1971). One would expect this kind of role strain to act negatively upon the woman's future advancement. The careers of these two women show no evidence of that. One will soon retire and the other has attained a considerably more influential position since 1974.

I do not claim the other women experienced no inner conflict about their role. Most did. Two "Mamas" discussed this. They both say they felt "slightly apologetic" at some time. In one instance these feelings may have been related to role learning, since they occurred early in the woman's career.

> I was awkward about it at the beginning. I was very
> cautious. Not wanting to push. It was a big handicap
> to me at the beginning. But I got over it when I
> realized it was silly.

What helped you see the fallacy of that?

> (pause) The problem with having this kind of discussion
> is that you end up sounding self-aggrandizing. It's hard
> for me to say that in the end I realized I knew better
> than a lot of people . . .

She still sounds apologetic. But she says she does not worry about what people think now, and the problem is "in her head." Observation confirmed this assessment. Another "Mama" suffered from similar feelings when certain people challenged her authority.

> There were those where my being the boss was challenged
> every inch of the way. In those instances I was frequently
> thrown off stride and found myself either overreacting or
> over-apologetic or overwilling to give in or move away
> rather than -- to avoid conflict . . . I used to go through
> the tortures of hell in how to handle those who challenged
> me.

She advises other women not to be apologetic -- to accept leadership as "your right." "My big problem was questioning it _myself._"

The temporary internal problems of these two women have not affected their style very much in my opinion. They continue to act as strong mother-leaders. They are satisfied with their style. Perhaps, too, a _motherly_ leadership style more easily accommodates occasional inner conflict and apologeticness than a stereotypical "male" leadership style. The female Type II leader must always feel a sense of failure if she betrays any of the stereotypical "female" traits. "Mamas" are largely spared this particular emotional problem.

One woman does not easily fall into any of the three categories I have described. She is a modern feminist. I think her understanding about the usual antagonistic relationship between female stereotypes and leadership influenced her response.

> I don't know that I'm a mother in the sense that a lot of
> people ascribe to the mother role, mother-figure, mother
> image. I really don't see that in myself . . .

> I'm too strong a person to really be mother. Most mothers
> are not really that strong personality. They are in a dif-
> ferent way. But I'm too out-front strong a person. I'm not
> the traditional mother type.

She perceived her own mother as "trapped" and relatively weak. Perhaps this childhood experience and her reading of feminist literature combine to turn her against the role, though there are indications that, if she would allow it, a Mama role would fall easily into place around her style of leadership.

She strongly encourages people of all ranks to call her by her first name. She "hates" formality. She referred to men and women callers on the phone and to her secretary as "Sweety" and "Dear." She displays her love for jewelry and perfume. She describes her relationships with people as being

"sincere, warm, and friendly."

> I've had people (staff) come in and discuss their personal
> problems with me, but I don't think it's in a motherly
> way. I think it's more that I'm receptive. I've had guys
> come in that are my contemporaries.

She implies that if her age-contemporaries seek her advice, that counterindicates

a motherly relationship.

> I have attracted some men who are not as strong as they
> might be. And I think they are looking for a woman who
> has the strength to solve their problems . . . There are
> men who are comfortable with strong women. I have
> attracted men like that. There's no question about it.

Like "Mamas" she stresses "dedication beyond the position itself" as her princi-

pal orientation to work. Like "Mamas," she attempts to "relax" men who feel

awkward about dealing with a woman in her position. "I recognize that they have

a problem, and I set them at ease." She jokes and laughs a lot. She shows her

emotions, "blows her stack."

> I voom and then I settle back into the routine, real fast.
> I am not a person to hold a grudge. I get it out in a
> hurry . . . I don't like to put people down . . . I don't
> function that way.

How does she get people to perform?

> I try to be personal in appreciating what they do. If they
> look nice or do a good job, I tell them.

She believes women have special talents that make them good administrators.

They have "more concern about people's feelings (than men). We deal with

people a lot."

Like the "Mamas," she draws no hard line between her experience as

a mother and her relations with people on the job.

I think being a mother sort of helps in understanding
people. And I think you can learn a lot from kids. You
can tell when people are lying, when they are telling the
truth. Kids are past masters at that. They cut through
a lot of chaff and get to the wheat when they are talking
about things. They're not as devious. I have learned a
lot from kids. Also you learn a degree of patience; you
learn to compromise; you learn to be a little more relaxed,
not quite so rigid. You learn a lot of things from being a
mother. There's no reason why fathers shouldn't learn
the same things, except they just don't have the contact
with their children.

Like the most outstanding of the "Mamas," she considers herself "part of a group

of people on their way to do good things. Common interests, goals." She does

not see herself as the leader carrying out specified functions and directing people

from a position of lonely isolation.

This relatively young woman has held her post the least time compared

to the other informants. There is no hesitancy in her style. She radiates confi-

dence, saying at different points in the interview, "I'm good (at my work)."

"I'm friendly." "I am a born leader." "I'm aggressive." "I am respected."

Understandably, she will not identify herself with what in America is often seen

as a weak image -- mother. This impressive and authoritative woman cannot be

styled as "Mama," "One of the Men" or "Orphan Annie." She may represent

younger women who will take more positions of leadership in the future. In her

style I see the most effective of the "Mama" techniques absent the ethnic over-

tones, the occasional apologeticness, the slight tendency to overwork and under-

delegate, the lingering feelings of status deprivation due to education or social

background. This particular woman warmly and easily combines traditionally

female superordinate interaction patterns with the self-assertion necessary to

lead people effectively.

SUMMARY TO LEADERSHIP TYPES

Traits of Type I Leaders

1. Developing people's potentials as the principal means of increasing production.

2. Hiring and assigning jobs by "chemistry."

3. Strategies designed to increase informality and deemphasize the heirarchy:

    a. Everyone goes by first name.

    b. Pronounced tendency to address people as Dear, Sweety-pie, Poor Baby, Love, and Hon.

    c. Arriving early to chat with people, getting involved with their personal problems.

    d. Hand clasping, hugging, patting, and walking arm-in-arm with people of all social ranks.

    e. Extensive use of humor to "relax people" and ease tensions.

4. Special ways of relating to people who are prejudiced against her, designed to "win them over."

5. Tendency to develop a "following" among workers and former workers.

6. Showing emotion, both hot and cold.

7. Tendency to use flamboyant language and talk loudly.

8. Thinks of herself as more devoted to the organization or the "cause" than as filling an office.

Traits of Type II Leaders

1. Increasing production, by whatever means, the main goal.

2. Comfortable with formality.

3. No special strategies for handling people other than what is formalized by the organization.

4. More likely to talk about "doing the job the best way possible" than being devoted to a "cause."

5. Tendency to hide some emotions.

6. Uses perceived male standards of behavior when in doubt. Wants to be treated and judged "same as a man."

7. Little bodily contact.

8. Maintains social distance.

9. Does not typically discuss personal problems with coworkers or subordinates.

Orphan Annie

1. Attempts to act and be perceived in Type II fashion, but does not "pull it off" as well as desired. Also uses some Type I techniques.

2. People respond in unwanted ways.

More women in this elite group (seven) can be described as Type I leaders. Six attempt to behave in Type II fashion, though two experience fairly serious problems in carrying it out. Both styles appear to promote production. Type I informants tell many stories about how men and women say they enjoy working with them and under them. They resemble successful "relationship-oriented" leaders. (Fiedler, 1971) Type II leaders are also successful by their own standards -- resembling "task-oriented" leaders.

Chart 3

INTERACTION STYLE

Success	Type I Female Styles	Type II Male Style
+	Mama, Teacher	One of the Men
-	Occasional Apologeticness, Self-doubt	Orphan Annie

COMMON GROUND

I have emphasized differences between the fourteen women leaders.
There are also similarities and many areas of agreement. The following are
some of the most notable areas of agreement:

1. Authority vested in the office accounts for much of the respect a woman leader
    is accorded.

Attempting to interpret the mothering ideology, I may have over-
emphasized the "need" of women to bolster their authority.

Type II politician:

> I essentially have control over what committees they
> serve on (colleagues) . . . They know that I'm a conse-
> quential vote. They do very much better with me on
> their side. (smile)

Type II administrator:

> You'd be surprised how many people will accept you in an
> upper position that would never accept you in a middle
> position.

Type I administrator:

Well, they haven't got the choice!

You have clout over them?

That's right. (laughter) That makes a great believer.

Type I administrator:

> I think a high position, especially in public life, com-
> mands a certain respect. I think people give that respect
> to the office. Probably that's a reason. And, being
> elected, my people accepted me . . .

Type I administrator:

> I go to them very honestly and say, "This is what (the
> elected official) wants, and this is how we have to move
> it . . ." They don't seem to be threatened by me. Nobody
> else can figure out why.

She invokes the name of a powerful man at whose pleasure some of them serve,

thus emphasizing her own position, which is at his right hand.

2. Doing things for subordinates is an important activity.

Blau (1964) writes that much of the authority of people in power is

accorded to them in exchange for services. The women who talked about doing

things for subordinates or constituents (nearly all of them), felt they do more

"favors" than their predecessors did. This was true among both types of leaders.

Administrators say they worked much harder than their predecessors for

salaries and advancement of subordinates. Politicians say they worked harder

for constituents. In Blau's scheme, this could mean that, in exchange for

authority, women invest in more favors than men. In other words, power costs

them more. I asked a Type II administrator,

Do you reward people for doing a good job?

> Compliments. And I have recommended them for jobs out-
> side the organization. I have fought for better salaries.

<u>Did your predecessor do this?</u>

No. On the contrary.

In some cases doing "favors" for subordinates is very time-consuming. A Type I administrator says,

> I have given the highest amount of outstanding appraisals, quality increases, step increases, of anybody (in the organization). This is a very time-consuming thing. To write one appraisal to get a quality increase takes you about a week. By recognizing them monetarily, they know that my thanks is sincere. They've helped me (get awards and promotions), now I'm willing to help them . . . Verbal thanks get nowhere.

<u>It's nice that (in your organization) there are set ways of rewarding people.</u>

> That's right. Out in (other organizations) they end up spending a lot of their own money buying gifts for people in thanks, which really is not a great deal of recognition. Giving them a quality increase means something to them in monthly pay, in retirement.

I feel this line of analysis deserves more attention in a more comprehensive study.

3. Accessibility was mentioned in one way or another by all informants.

Allowing me to interview them is, of course, a measure of their accessibility. Two business leaders, mentioned earlier, were not accessible to me, indicating that accessibility is not a universal trait among women leaders. In retrospect I am astounded at the access the others allowed. Nearly all informants said that, in their estimation, woman leaders are more accessible than men.

> I am more open to constituents (than predecessor) . . . Of course, you have to remember we (women) are accessible.

113

A lot of people call me and say, "You're not my (representative), but I feel more comfortable talking to you."
Or, "Can I come in and talk to you first" -- they're
afraid to call their male (representative).

It's a little like talking to mother first, before father?

Yeah. Sort of. I've had that happen so many times!
. . . I get ten times as many calls as the men. I take
it as a compliment.

Are there any advantages in being a woman?

No. (pause) Excuse me, I should qualify that. I think
one advantage is that people seem to feel that I'm more
easily approached. They don't see me as untouchable.
Even if they do at first, when we talk over their problems,
they seem to feel more comfortable with me (than the men).

And of course my door is always open. People can reach
me. I like that. I want to be where I can be reached. I
don't want to ever be shut off.

I notice that the men deal with (military man with approxi-
mately the same status and function) with more tenterhooks
. . . They expect that they have to treat him as -- with
formality. He resents it. There's a lot they won't tell
him. With me, we get right into the meat and potatoes.

High evaluation of accessibility in leadership seems to have little

relationship to leadership style.

4.   Contrary to some speculations, I found no Queen Bees.

A recent article in a popular periodical inferred (from the results of

a mail-in questionnaire) that successful career women discourage competition

from their own kind. (Staines, et al, 1974) Without exception, my informants

have encouraged and helped other women. They serve on committees that ad-

vance women; several routinely urge competent women subordinates to work

elsewhere if the advantages are greater there. Leaders of both styles typically

"groom" competent women subordinates for higher positions. A common remark of these leaders is that woman bosses or politicians are especially accessible to women, or that women in particular feel comfortable working for them.

These leaders are well informed on women's issues and would like to see women taking 50% or _more_ of administrative and leadership positions, reflecting women's representation in the organization or constituency. As a group, they feel more competent and able than their male predecessors. Many of them believe women have something _more_ to offer -- that the world would benefit by having more of them in positions of power. They typically dislike the idea of preferential hiring, however, because that violates their keen sense of work and accomplishment.

5. There was near unanimity that female experience as mother and low-level worker enhances woman's leadership abilities.

This Type I leader's response is typical:

How do you get the respect and loyalty of workers?

> I have always liked people immensely. And having worked all my life, I have great respect for the job that the workers down below the top level do. Somehow they realize that, maybe by my response or whatever.

Women who worked their way up from the bottom feel that administrators coming in at the top will "lose something."

Asked if her experience as a mother helps her, the following informant gives a typical response.

> Yes. I have a profound empathy for young people . . . I think it sort of helps in understanding people, and I think you can learn a lot from kids.

Type II leaders and "orphans" are slightly less likely to value motherhood experience. But they value it nevertheless.

I'm sure it has (helped). Anybody's experience in
anything along the way helps.

A Type II leader who is childless says, "Obviously one's experience in anything
is useful."

American women often feel that their everyday experiences count for
nothing in the worlds of business and politics. The women I interviewed do not
agree. A highly successful entrepreneur says that her experience as a mother
was directly responsible for the ideas behind her most successful products. She
believes her womanly talents in "reading people" helped her market the products
and helped her attain and maintain contacts with important accounts. Additionally,
being a woman has been extremely useful in advertising the products. She reminds us that --

The consumers are primarily women . . . Women spend
most of the money. Men try to second guess how a woman's
mind works. Very often they (don't succeed). Thus you
have sexism in advertising, which is very offensive . . .

If this study is indicative, women in leadership positions do not de-
value experiences gained in the performance of lower level, traditionally
"female" work.

EPILOGUE

The majority of these fourteen women grew up in lower-middle level socioeconomic households. They were not spoonfed advantages of middle class life. They walked miles, worked after school, and often helped their fathers support the family. But socioeconomic status in itself may not be the most important factor in terms of development of a positive self-image. On the contrary, most literature associates lower status with poor self-image. What emerges here as the crucial factor in the majority of cases -- and in every case in which the woman has attained a very high degree of power -- is a strong mother with whom the daughter identifies. Middle-lower to lower socioeconomic status may facilitate mothers' expression of strength. Regardless of class, perceiving their mother as an instrumental, community, cultural, or even household leader may help girls develop a positive, assertive self-definition. Most of the families were geographically and psychologically close.

Motivation to achieve appears to be related more to upholding family and cultural traditions, rather than a breaking away from tradition or discovery of a "new way."

The great majority were "marginal" in the sense that they felt different from average children. By their recollections they received much typical female socialization. In addition to this, they learned to compete and play in groups with boys, a fact they believe to be important in their ability to work with men on an equal footing. They typically had few aspirations other than to be independent and to do a good job wherever they are.

In her review of Fogarty's Women in Top Jobs, Epstein (1973) writes:

> Women who rise to the top often get there because of
> chance, the crisis of war which creates a demand for
> personpower (<u>man</u>power being off at war), the death of
> a relative. One sees that many women who assume
> directorship roles under these conditions would not
> have sought them under normal circumstances. (p. 288)

I doubt this conclusion. The experiences of most of my informants led me to view chance as a relatively minor factor. In any case, resolution of this point must depend on a comparative analysis between males and females in top jobs. The women included in this analysis all passed through a series of demanding tests of ability, fortitude, and loyalty. Whether paid or unpaid, they spiraled upwards because they achieved recognition for those qualities, often surmounting male prejudice. To attribute this achievement largely to "chance" downgrades their personal contributions. Looking at career spirals as I have done should cast doubt on the common assumption that, by itself, "working harder than a man" or "three times as hard as a man" explains women's successful careers. Other factors are also important. In addition, not all womanly traits work against advancement.

Once in a top job, accumulated visibility from successive stages of their careers provides women with the respect of their subordinates and colleagues. The authority vested in their offices increases their prestige. But leadership style or technique of interacting with coworkers appears to add another dimension to their authority. Half of the women blended two supposedly incompatible statuses -- woman and leader -- invoking a mother-like authority. Coworkers appear to participate in the creation of this mother role. Where it is fully developed, workers and leader alike feel comfortable and production is reportedly high. In a practical sense, this means women need not "become like men" to be effective.

Several other informants are guided by their perception of male inter-action style. Instead of "developing people" as a means to production, they achieve production by whatever means is necessary. This "traditional" or "task-oriented" leadership style can be highly effective for women, but it appears to be more difficult for some to play. Two of the women who emulate male interaction styles appeared to experience more difficulty in achieving a sense of authority, as they would define it.

Fiedler's interesting analysis of situational components of effective leadership concludes that --

> . . . task-motivated leaders tended to perform better than relationship-motivated leaders in very favorable and in relatively unfavorable situations. (A highly structured situation in which subordinates are totally dependent on leader for advancement is a "favorable" situation. A life and death crisis is an "unfavorable" situation.) The relationship-motivated leaders tended to perform better than task-motivated leaders in situations of intermediate favorableness. (1971, p. 13)

In today's world, where employee rights and authority diffusion increase, situations are moving from highly favorable to intermediate favorableness. In politics the same trend is occurring for different reasons. Under these circumstances, many female leaders should be effective. Even Type II woman leaders may be more relationship-oriented than their male predecessors. *

---

* Perhaps Fiedler's definition of favorableness grows out of a male perspective.

During "unfavorable situations" survival depends on working together. People are apparently willing to forego pleasant relationships to rally behind a "strong leader" of traditional masculine cast. Life and death situations, like highly favorable situations, are becoming rarer. If these assessments are accurate, women's talents in administration and politics should find fertile situational soil in the years ahead.

Management schools today appear to be responding to a change in organizational environments. Recently much literature used in these schools stresses the importance of sensitivity to people and their problems. The entire field of management and leadership has been affected by the "human relations" movement. Although there is little hard evidence that changing a leader's style changes effectiveness (Fiedler, 1971; Stogdill, 1974), the push continues away from the cold, rational, "traditional" style of leadership epitomized by military officers.

Female socialization stresses sensitivity to people and their problems, to group identification more than autonomy. (Weitzman, 1975; Sears et al, 1957; and Lewis (1968) Due to their upbringing, woman leaders may find it easier to implement the "new" management techniques. The ironic fact is male leaders appear to be hard at work trying to learn a style of leadership that probably comes more easily to women.

APPENDIX

The following is my complete interview guide. Not all questions could be asked of all informants, as time limitation was sometimes a factor. Some information came from other, published interviews that focused on the same kinds of experiences. I did not follow the guide rigidly even when time was no factor. As noted in the Prologue, some of the principal concepts developed from probing in uncharted directions. Some of the questions were added after I had interviewed a few informants. For these reasons, the list should be regarded as a skeletal guide.

Interview Guide

Introduction

I assure you these tapes will be heard only by me. Then they will be destroyed after I have extracted the relevant data from them.

I will not disclose these confidences to anyone.

Specific information about incidents or people will only be used in the formation of more abstract ideas about working women.

When my report is finished, your name and the name of your organization will be omitted. The identity of your organization will be masked in generalities.

The purpose of the study is to discover how successful women manage their lives, their work, and their relationships with others.

Face Sheet

How long in the organization?

Salary?

Marriage status?

Children?

Husband's occupation?

Position?

Education?

Ethnicity?

Extended family size?

Recency of immigration?

Work history?

Questions

Have you ever been afraid of becoming successful or influential?

What values or morals were emphasized in your family?

When you were a child, who in your family encouraged or influenced

you to do well?

Number of children in family of origin?

Ordinal number of position in family?

Size of extended family?

How far back were your ancestors immigrants?

When you were a child, were you acquainted with a woman who

worked?

In growing up, did you ever consciously tone down your desire to get

good grades?

How has your ethnic status affected you? (For women of distinct ethnic status)

How has being the daughter of an immigrant affected you? (For daughters of immigrants)

What training did you get in being feminine?

In your earliest years do you remember competing against a brother or a male relative?

What did you want to be when you grew up? earliest years? high school? later?

As a child were you a leader? How do you think you accomplished this?

In high school were you a leader?

Did you feel different from the average child? teenager?

Have you ever had the feeling that the "mantle of the family" was on your shoulders?

As a child or adolescent, what kind of marriage arrangement did you envisage as the ideal?

What type of boy did you typically date?

Do women get more acceptable as leaders the older they get?

Do you ever feel that being a woman gives you an advantage?

Do you have a working philosophy of life?

Is your general philosophy the same as your colleagues?

Describe the kind of life you see yourself living, if everything goes well in the future.

Can you describe any important "turning points" in your life being "taken seriously"?

Are there any areas that seem to be closed, or partly closed, to you simply because of your sex?

Who were the key people who facilitated your advancement to your present position?

How much education or experience was required for the job?

Describe a typical work day from beginning to end. Kinds of decisions?

How do you rate your ability to administer?

Do you think women generally have the qualities needed to supervise effectively?

In what ways are you similar to other women in your line of work?

Are there any feminine qualities that you think are beneficial in doing this work?

Are standards for your performance as high as for men? Higher? (Predecessors, if applies)

How would you describe the role your superior plays in the organization?

What kind of working relationship do you have with your immediate superior?

Do secretaries give you the same respect or service they give to men in your position?

Have you ever been responsible for getting anyone fired? Promoted?

What strategies do you use in giving direction to people of different ages?

Do you feel you would rather do work yourself, when you are able to do it well, even though that kind of work normally is done by a subordinate?

Has any man ever "come on" sexually while you were attempting to carry on business relations?

Does anyone try to cast you in the mother role?

Are you aware of any role you play in dealing with peers?

How do you usually react when a colleague takes the initiative on something which you thought was your prerogative?

Do your male peers extend you the usual courtesies -- opening doors, holding chairs, etc.?

What is your special imprint upon the office?

How do you handle disagreements with colleagues? How do you win them over?

How do you try to handle yourself when you have been praised in front of your peers?

Can you think of an example when a colleague refused to work with you?

When you first took over your present position, what tactics did you use to get people to respect you -- or to follow your directions?

Relationship with clients (people you seek to influence outside your organization).

Describe the typical tone of your meetings.

When you wish to influence people, do you offer to buy them coffee? Lunch?

Does being female provide a means of "breaking the ice" with some clients?

Do clients (constituents) commonly discuss with you their feelings about working with a woman?

Do you usually try to get on a first-name basis with people?

Have you consciously eliminated any relationships on account of working?

What type of consumer are you?

How has working affected your health?

What kinds of things does your husband expect of you as a wife?

Do your children like having a working mother?

Do you feel your children are missing out on some things because of having a working mother?

How does your husband feel about your working?

Does having a dirty house make you feel guilty or bad?

Who do your friends tend to be? working women? any non-working women? married, unmarried?

Do you encounter subtle resistance among your friends -- resistance to your working?

Do you think of yourself as a supporter of the woman's movement?

What things would you like to be able to do, but you find you have too little time?

126

Have I left anything out that you think is important in understanding

the real quality of your life?

REFERENCES

Blau, Peter. Exchange and Power in Social Life. New York, London and London and Sydney: John Wiley & Sons, 1964.

Bronfenbrenner, Urie. "Socialization and Social Class Through Time and Space." Readings in Social Psychology. Eleanor Maccoby, Theodore Newcomb, and Eugene Hartley (Eds.). Third edition. New York: Holt and Co., 1958, pp. 400-425.

-------------- "The Changing American Child -- A Speculative Analysis." In Edwards, John N. (Ed.) The Family and Change, pp. 236 - 250. Originally published 1961.

Constantini, Edmond and Kenneth H. Craik. "Women as Politicians: The Social Background, Personality, and Political Careers of Female Party Leaders." Journal of Social Issues. 28 (No. 2, 1972), 217-236.

Davis, Elizabeth Gould. The First Sex. Baltimore, Md.: Penguin Book, 1971.

Edwards, John N. (Ed.) The Family and Change. New York: Alfred A. Knopf, 1969.

Epstein, Cynthia Fuchs. Review of Fogarty, et al. Women in Top Jobs. In Social Forces. 52 (Dec. 1973), 288. Book published 1971.

-------------- Woman's Place: Options and Limits in Professional Careers. Berkeley, Los Angeles and London: University of California Press, 1971.

-------------- "Women vs Success." Intellectual Digest (Sept. 1973), 26.

Fiedler, Fred E. Leadership. Morristown, N. J.: General Learning Press, 1971.

Gerth, H. H. and C. Wright Mills. From Max Weber: Essays in Sociology. New York: Oxford University Press, 1948. Paperback reprint, 1969.

Goode, William. "A theory of Role Strain." American Sociological Review. 25 (August 1959), 38-47.

-------------- World Revolution and Family Patterns. New York: The Free Press, 1970. Paperback edition.

Hackett, Bruce. Higher Civil Servants in California. Institute of Governmental Studies: University of California, 1967.

Hartley, Ruth E. "Some Implications of Current Changes in Sex-Role Patterns." In Edwards, The Family and Change.

Homans, George C. The Human Group. New York: Harcourt, Brace, 1950.

Hughes, Everett. "Social Change and Status Protest: An Essay on the Marginal Man." Phylon. 10 (1949), 58-65.

Kammeyer, Kenneth. "Birth Order and the Feminine Sex Role Among College Women." American Sociological Review. 31 (1966), 508-515.

Klapp, Orrin E. Public Dramas and Public Men. Chicago: Aldine, 1965.

Kohn, Melvin L. Class and Conformity: A study in Values. Homewood, Ill.: The Dorsey Press, 1969.

Lee, Marcia M. "Towards Understanding Why Few Women Hold Public Office." Unpublished paper prepared for delivery at the 1974 Annual Meeting of the American Political Science Association. Copyright, 1974, The American Political Science Association.

Lewis, Edwin C. Developing Woman's Potential. Ames, Iowa: Iowa State University Press, 1968.

Lofland, John. Analyzing Social Settings. Belmont, Calif.: Wadsworth, 1971.

Merton, Robert K., George Reader, and Patricia Kendall (Eds.). Social Theory and Social Structure. Glencoe, Ill.: The Free Press, 1957.

Park, Rosemary. "Like Their Fathers Instead." Corporate Lib: Women's Challenge to Management. Baltimore and London: Johns Hopkins University Press, 1973. Pp. 39-57.

Parsons, Talcott and Robert F. Bales. Family, Socialization and Interaction Process. Glencoe, Ill.: The Free Press, 1955. Second printing.

Priest, Ivy Baker. Green Grows Ivy. New York, Toronto, London: McGraw-Hill, 1958.

Sears, Pauline, Eleanor Maccoby and Harry Levin. Patterns of Child Rearing. Evanston, Ill.: Row, Peterson, 1957.

Seeman, Melvin. Social Status and Leadership. Ohio State University: Bureau of Education Research and Service, 1960.

Staines, Graham, Carol Tavris, and Toby Epstein Jayarantne. "The Queen Bee Syndrome." Psychology Today. 7 (Jan. 1974), 55-60.

Stogdill, Ralph M. Handbook of Leadership. New York: The Free Press, 1974.

Strodtbeck, F. L. "Family Interaction, Values, and Achievement." In McClelland, D. et al. Talent and Society. Princeton, New Jersey: Van Nostrand, 1958, 135-194.

Tausky, Curt and Robert Dubin. "Career Anchorage: Managerial Mobility Motivations." American Sociological Review. 30 (Oct. 1965)

Wardwell, Walter. "A Marginal Professional Role: Chiropractor." Social Forces. 30 (March 1952), 339-348.

Weitzman, Lenore J. "Sex-Role Socialization." In Jo Freeman (Ed.). Women: A Feminist Perspective. State University of New York: Mayfield, 1975. Pp. 105-144.

Werner, Emmy E. "Women in the State Legislatures." Western Political Quarterly. 21 (March 1968), 40-50.

West, Naida S. Social Characteristics of the Preschool Staff and Value Orientation. Unpublished M. A. thesis, Sacramento State College, 1971.

Rosen, B. L. and D'Andrade, R. "The Psychosocial Origins of Achievement Motivation." Sociometry. 22 (1959), 185-217.